PORTRAIT SERIES

Aspects of Buses

by
D.D. Gladwin

THE OAKWOOD PRESS

© Oakwood Press & D.D. Gladwin 2003

British Library Cataloguing in Publication Data
A Record for this book is available from the British Library
ISBN 0 85361 607 8

Typeset by Oakwood Graphics.
Repro by Ford Graphics, Ringwood, Hants.
Printed by Cambrian Printers, Aberystwyth, Ceredigion.

Above: Difficult to tell if the cartoonist was being unkind to your author or not! Gloomily I must admit opinion claims he was all too accurate. But my shoes always shone!

Title page: The worried face of the 1930s, the driver, of course, the Leyland Tiger merely snarled.

Rear cover, top: York Pullman Bus Co. Ltd AEC Regal III single-decker No. 59 FVY 411 on the south side service at Piccadilly bus stand in May 1969. *Keith Turns*

Rear cover, bottom: Full-fronted double-decker No. 36 HAA 771E had a Deutz air-cooled engine on a Guy Arab II chassis of 1944 vintage, with Reading Coachworks bodywork. It is seen at Gosport ferry in June 1970. *Keith Turns*

Published by The Oakwood Press (Usk), P.O. Box 13, Usk, Mon., NP15 1YS.
E-mail: oakwood-press@dial.pipex.com
Website: www.oakwood-press.dial.pipex.com

Contents

Introduction 5

Days with a Horse 12

Steam Transcendent 20

Petrol Precursors 22

The 1920s Learning Curve 28

Reduction through Regulation - The 1930s 49

Entrenchment through War 73

Bus Resurgent - The 1940s 81

The Golden Age of the '50s 91

The Colours of Pride 113

The Swinging Sixties 129

The Sober Seventies 145

Bus Descendent - The 1980s 167

In Vogue - The Mini 184

New Age, New Ways - The 1990s 188

Acknowledgements 206

Index 207

Author's Note

The illustrations used in this book are intended to show many of the facets of bus life and necessarily come from a wide variety of sources. In more than a few cases where an appeal was made to a colleague for help even where they could not supply any illustrations directly they suggested alternatives, usually enhancing the selection.

Photographs are credited where I know, or can track down or guess, the source but any missing copyright acknowledgements that are notified will gladly be corrected in a later edition.

In 1956 a Company Chairman of the old fashioned sort wrote: 'Urban transport must be frequent, speedy, and clean, and as cheap as possible, consistent with good wages and conditions of service and a high standard of maintenance. Above all, our service must be given pleasantly . . .' That is what most busmen and women did and do, and it is no bad thing to be proud of.

'Move along the car please, there will [still] be another one along soon!'

What is a 'typical' bus? In a historical sense this must be it. An AEC Regent 9613A chassis with 9.6 litre engine, 'crash' gearbox and 56-seat bodywork by Crossley of Errwood Park, A778 entered service in 1951 with Liverpool Corporation Transport, had a 15 year life and, as can be seen from the photograph, looked 'right'. Included in the first 8 ft wide batch of buses delivered to Liverpool, the blinds are clear, the radiator polished, the driver uniformed and the paintwork (green and cream) although stained has been washed. Add to this a magnificent amalgam of 1950s city scenery, tramrails, cobbles, soot-blackened buildings and (it being January) a 'clemmed' atmosphere and you have the pure essence of city-bus, rivalling any inferior perfume.

Introduction

The title of this book is as accurate as can be, but within the covers will be found photographs of a few true coaches as well as a number of those heterogeneous vehicles, the 'boach' or 'cus', having either a coach body with bus seats, or being demoted coaches seeing out their days typically carrying schoolchildren, groceries or tinkers. There is also the problem of definition as the question arises of whether or not services operated by National Express are, despite the use of often extremely luxurious coaches, nothing more or less than long bus journeys. Years ago when Green Line Coaches were a prestigious part of London Transport's manifold activities, overcrowding could lead to ordinary service buses making an appearance. On one never-to-be-forgotten day a wartime Daimler ran on Route 722 complete with wooden seats - but officially, and painted as a Green Line vehicle!

During the preliminary discussions over the book's content publisher Jane Kennedy specifically asked me to travel down a busman's memories, memories of the byways of operation, with a sideways look at some of the plain eccentricities that have graced Public Service Vehicle life. There are, too, a handful of vehicles destined to 'go foreign' which can raise questions of their own - for example, did any of the Leylands exported to Baghdad survive the war? Did the dragon which is reputed to have run round a bus on Westminster Bridge go with it to Kowloon, or was it merely Mr Ping of the Mandarin Chop Suey House in disguise?

Quite a few of the photographs are chosen to allow the reader to wallow in nostalgia, for there is something quite heart-jerking when one views the scenes of buses in the old days. Conditions were, of course, quite apalling and vehicles were all too often built with little or no thought for either bus crews or maintenance staff. A hand-operated controller and hand brake are fine on a tram, but pity the trolleybus driver who had also to twissle the wheel in order to get his narrow solid tyres away from a lethal combination of oil, grease, horse muck, steel tram rails and cobbles.

Mind you, one feels a perceptive pre-World War I comment by A.H. Pott, of the Metropolitan Electric Tramways Ltd, was also slightly tongue-in-cheek when he wrote that: 'The leading feature of omnibuses, of whatever class, is their great mobility as compared with tramways or trolley buses. Not only can they thread their way through vehicular traffic more easily, but every vehicle is independent of another, and it is probably the skill with which the drivers dodge pedestrian and vehicular traffic which makes the bus popular by adding zest to the ride, especially when skidding on greasy roads'.

And the country busman - or bus person - had problems of their own. When I was with Midland Red one year, just before Christmas, I had to follow a traction engine and all his threshing paraphenalia at a steady 5 mph for two miles with a radiator hissing and gurgling in front of my nose and then still had to recover the lost time as the Post Office 'In Town' closed at 1 pm for its half day and it wouldn't do for the pensioners to miss the visit. Then with a private concern, Beryl, one of our girls, once broke off the gear lever in her old Commer, drove about 10 miles jammed in second, reached the yard, threw the broken length of steel at me and, laughing happily, declared it 'were real beggar, lad' while her passengers cheered!

Conversely, remember vacuum-operated windscreen wipers? The slower you went, the slower they went. Add driving snow on the uplands of Derbyshire and a slack fan belt allowing the dynamo to slip, and the cinema return trip became a battle. Mind we nearly always got there. Not because I and my colleagues were the

'Company's Servants', as the Rulebook said, but because we had an obligation to do all we could to carry passengers where and when they wanted to go. That they left us preferring the supposed security and reliability of their cars is history, but hardly the fault of the men and women who worked hard and enthusiastically within the industry.

For years Corporation treasurers accepted that certain routes were very profitable and understood that some services met a social need even if they ran at a loss. Excess profits, i.e. those over and above running costs and reasonable fleet renewals, went to help the rates. The whole history of British bus work has also relied on private entrepreneurs who would run services that never had a chance to pay even direct costs but which might lead to a private hire or perhaps a handful of tour bookings. None of those honourable men and women ever seem to have checked whether this was so, but as long as wages got paid and they made a bob or two they were quite content to plod on, buying tidy second-hand buses and coaches from the 'big boys' who sold them off after a relatively short life. There was, and still is, also a type of man or woman who was willing to put up with low (and sometimes late) wages and of whom the Transport & General Workers Union despaired, fulminating that their acceptance of poor wages and conditions depressed those of the whole industry.

But can this last? The new giant concerns do not cascade their vehicles until they are almost scrap and when the small operator has gone what will happen to the less viable routes? Already councils face quite hefty subsidy bills, and as they have more and more calls on their available income, quite what can be done to preserve rural, unremunerative services is difficult to see. The big companies are run by a breed of accountant whose attitude is that loss-making bus services are not their problem, one such telling me one day that the logical step is for the Government to sell a car to each rural family at rock-bottom prices and to abandon country buses. Arguments against this attitude are weakened by the incontrovertible facts that, driving a bus, one regularly sees would-be passengers being given a lift by helpful neighbours and even pensioners are 'pooling' the cost of a taxi rather than carrying their shopping from the nearest bus stop.

HHB 184K has an East Lancs body, designed for one-person-operation and is seen when new in 1972 while in service with Merthyr Tydfil Corporation. The chassis is a Leyland Leopard.   *E.V. Trigg*

For practical purposes, other than the expensive Metro tramways being built in major cities, there is no easily available alternative to the diesel-engined bus, although a workable trolley/diesel hybrid has been developed in Europe. It was not always so as in 1912 a table appeared in a serious journal giving corrected (and comparable) costs for all three forms of road transport - the bus, the tram and the trolleybus.

	Tramway	Omnibus	Railless Traction
	Cost per tram mile	Cost per bus mile	Cost per bus mile
	d.	d.	d.
Power	1.00	-	.66
Petrol	-	.70	-
Distribution { Overhead equipment, Cables }	.14	-	.14
Repairs of cars			
Electrical equipment or engines	.15	.25 }	} .30
Truck repairs	.18	.50 }	
Tyres	-	1.00	1.00
Bodies and paint	.16	.30	.20
Permanent Way repairs	.14	-	-
Buildings repair and maintenance	.02	.01	.02
Running	2.70	2.62	2.40
Administration }		.75	
Insurance }	.70	1.00	
Rates and taxes	.07	.12	} .75
Renewals	.10	-	
Licences	.01	.07 }	
Accidents	.16	.40	.10
Interest on capital	1.44	.40	.49
Total cost per car mile	6.97	7.22	6.06

This made the demand for trolleybuses ('Railless Traction') all the more reasonable as, although there were many problems with these, they were perceived as quiet and fume free.

The speed at which the motor bus entered service in London was nothing short of miraculous; by 1908 vehicles nominally in service totalled 1,075, spread around 40 manufacturers. Taking only those that reached double figures we find names long forgotten, while others either extant today or only recently expired included Maudslay (6), Dennis (6), Brush (4) and Thornycroft (3). Eighteen manufacturers made a respectable initial showing, but most petered out quite quickly. The figures show the maximum number of each maker's vehicles registered at any time within the year, but probably only 50 per cent would be available for work.

	1905	1906	1907	1908
Straker-Squire (including Büssing)	27	217	344	358
Milnes-Daimler	99	244	322	312
De Dion et Bouton	9	103	162	174
Wolseley	4	4	54	80
Arrol-Johnston	-	1	7	30
Dürkopp	22	32	31	17
Leyland	8	14	10	15
Armstrong-Whitworth	-	-	4	10
Lacoste et Battman	-	29	29	1
Scott Stirling	12	57	67	-
Eugène Brillié	2	16	15	-
Scheibier	1	20	21	-
Orion	5	11	9	-
Ducommun	-	10	-	-
Germain	14	13	-	-
Steam				
Darracq-Serpollet	-	-	10	20
Clarkson	2	43	46	15
Electric				
Electrobus	-	-	7	15

The history of the British bus industry has, to a very large extent, also been the history of many commercial vehicle manufacturers. Makers of chassis and bodywork alike have come and gone, with some backing the wrong mechanical horse, others, especially coachbuilders, wandering off to do their own, often idiosyncratic, thing, with many scuttling back too late to nice prosaic vehicle designs when their customers demanded the outlines and styles they knew. In very many instances a Corporation bus fleet manager would buy a good solid chassis from Daimler, AEC or Leyland, more or less the same as that delivered the year before and the year before that, only varying the bodywork if the price made the preferred bodywork too expensive for the Corporation Treasurer. Some quoted prices, especially in the 1930s, reflected the coachbuilders' fears that they might lose orders, such jobs being undertaken at cost. The only change would come when a new manager was appointed who might have ideas of his own from previous experience, or alternatively where a company demonstration vehicle might prove beyond doubt that the time had come to change. There were, however, two twists to this scenario, the first being that some managers came and went suspiciously quickly, often not appearing in that position again, or that the demonstrator, which after all rarely stayed more than a week or two, was a false prophet and myriad nastinesses would surface after a few months - or more often days - after the guarantee ran out . . .

Seating on buses has long been a remarkably overlooked subject. In general manufacturers have been torn between the often conflicting requirements of comfort, legroom, easy accessibility, weight, durability and security. Vehicle design constraints have always affected one or more of these. An obvious example was that mobile nastiness, the lowheight double-decker commonly used before the new 1960s designs became widespread, where access to the four-in-a-row banks of upstairs seats was via an offset sunken trough. Each row of seats was higher than this trough and a step up was required, while in the lower saloon this trough being above the seats ensured not a few cracked skulls.

As a schoolboy part of my journey involved Eastern National Bristols which had just this style of bodywork. I invite you to imagine a scenario where, having got pinned on the inside, a small schoolboy had as his neighbours a large lady, dressed all in black complete with oilskin shopping bag, and outboard of her two large pipe-smoking dockers who had been frequenting the Mariner's Arms, one of the few pubs then open all day. The bell-push to stop the bus is by the trough. Did I - dare I - ask the other three to move, would they move in time for me to ding the bell to stop the bus where I wanted to get off, or was it better to go on to the terminus and hope the conductor would believe my story? Mind you, at the terminus there were always lots of collectible tickets . . !

Interior lighting is another aspect of travel where relatively poor equipment was the norm for many years. The replacement of tungsten bulbs with fluorescents makes reading more practicable although its harshness does little to flatter girls' complexions. On the other hand during the war, only minimal lighting both inside and out was allowed as keen-eyed Luftwaffe pilots might see and bomb a bus. Incredible as it may seem now the clippie was expected to issue tickets either by touch or with a pen-light torch. Some passengers, particularly foreigners after the Dunkirk exodus, were unscrupulous enough to pass 'dud' or foreign coins for their fares trusting they would be undetected - but this lost money was promptly stopped from the clippies' wages.

Aspects of wartime bus work cannot by their nature show much of the heroism and devotion to work by the majority of crews, both in cities and country they faced quite dreadful conditions. Although not entirely typical one of our neighbours came home after a 12-hour shift to find his house 'doodle-bugged', luckily his family survived but he had to go back on duty the same evening. Another driver in Essex, riding his bicycle home, was hospitalized by a drunken US Army lorry-driver - no compensation was offered or paid. And for this drivers and conductors alike were abused, spat at and attacked for being civilians.

Two 1942 aspects of wartime bus work show just how different the world was then. An 18-year-old youth was accused of insulting behaviour and remanded in custody for 'refusing to take his place in a bus queue'. It was said 'he placed himself at the head of a queue of over one hundred', refused to move and was accordingly arrested.

By contrast it was reported that several members of the Institute of Transport in the prisoner-of-war camps Oflag VI B and Stalag XX A had formed themselves into study groups and were allowed by the Germans (who had permitted correspondence courses and books to be supplied) to take their examinations as though in the UK.

Wartime propoganda permeated most timetables, and as late as 1944 homilies included 'Are you a member of a War Savings Group? If not - join one now'; 'Save and Lend - for Hitler's End'; 'All clear for Savings'; 'Lend freely - to live freely'; 'Saving is your "plane" duty' and 'Pilot your savings to victory'.

<u>DON'T</u> HINDER THE WAR EFFORT BY
TRAVELLING NEEDLESSLY
<u>DO</u> HELP IT BY REGULARLY BUYING
SAVINGS CERTIFICATES

Provision of bus stops, bus shelters and bus stations has long been a bone of contention between operator, councils and users. Obviously the operator wants to provide some information, if only a basic timetable, but traditionally used the Post Office, public house or village green notice boards for this. Councils would like all stops to be highly visible with updated route timings clearly displayed, while the public (and especially those who only use the bus when the car is in for servicing or during mid-winter when they perceive road conditions are too bad for driving) seemingly want centrally heated waiting rooms with newspapers. All this for their £1 fare! The reality is that most villages will have a shelter with, if not vandalized, a timetable. Elsewhere it all depends where you live. One Border town with 22,000 population has totally unmarked pick-up points, the location of which had to be ascertained from a schoolgirl, whereas in South Yorkshire the most obscure stop seems to have sprouted a totem pole.

In this book there are no photographs of accidents involving injury but one of the most interesting sets of illustrations show a Leyland National being tested to destruction in a simulated accident; such tests on PSVs, mainly because of cost, were rare. Accidents have many causes, in my case varying from unpleasant to downright farcical; in Glasgow during 1949 when collating statistics the General Manager pointed out that one accident could be a driver's mirror being knocked off and another injure 50 passengers, but for what they were worth quoted the following:

Types of Accidents	Tramcars	Motorbuses	Trolley buses
	%	%	%
Boarding	11	5	33
Leaving	10	3	9
Knocked down	8	12	12
Collision	61	69	23
Miscellaneous	5	1	4
On vehicle	5	10	19
	100	100	100

No doubt, and here I can see drivers of all ages nodding their heads in agreement, the main enemy is the pedestrian. Not because they are pedestrians (we all are sometime) but because all too often they are oblivious to the looming bulk of a bus bearing down on them. Worse still halfway to the other side, and still ignoring that great big red bus, they turn around and retrace their steps.

In 1950, H. Muscroft, the General Manager of Huddersfield's fleet, summed up the probable result:

> Here lies the body of Timothy Gray,
> Who died asserting his right of way,
> He was right, quite right,
> But the bus sped on,
> And Timothy Gray is just as dead as if he were wrong.

A major problem found with driver-only buses is that service to the public has necessarily deteriorated, not only because there is no longer anyone to chat to, but because the hitherto idle time when a driver was waiting for the bell is occupied by the often stressful gathering of fares and the asociated ticket issuing. It all adds up to a far less relaxing environment and, given some of the diagrams where a four minute break every hour is a good day, there can be no contrast with, for example, our old Warwick-Leamington circuits. There was precious little spare time at either end but, and it was a big but, the conductor could dive over to the cafe and come back with two steaming mugs of tea and lardy cakes. One side effect of this relatively civilized way of life was that not only could the conductor direct passengers to their destinations, help them with shopping, prams, and all the other impedimenta that housewives (and others) seem to carry with them, but he or she could if it was their nature, act as entertainers. Bus crews had a true sense of humour and I always remember when travelling as a passenger 40 years ago talking to a driver about his days in Southport. On one occasion they were passing the cemetery and the elderly conductor was collecting the 1d. fares. 'Any more fares, if you please, lals and gennelmen, any more fares?' After a pause, 'Have you seen that wall, lals and gennelmen? Funny old place that as nobody seems to come out and, bless them, nobody wants to go in, so why put a wall around a cemetery?'

PRIVATE OMNIBUSES FOR FAMILY PARTIES
TRAVELLING BY
GREAT WESTERN RAILWAY.

The Great Western Company provide Omnibuses to and from the PADDINGTON STATION, capable of conveying SIX PERSONS INSIDE and TWO OUTSIDE, with the usual quantity of luggage.

To avoid disappointment, these vehicles should be ENGAGED BEFOREHAND, and should there at any time be more orders than can be executed with the number of vehicles at disposal, such orders will be dealt with according to priority.

Parties LEAVING LONDON and requiring to proceed to PADDINGTON STATION from their Residences or Hotels should give TWELVE HOURS' NOTICE, addressed to the Station Master, Paddington Station, W., stating the date, and likewise the train by which they intend to leave Paddington.

Parties intending to PROCEED TO LONDON from Country Stations should give 24 hours' notice, either at the Station from which they will start, or to the Station Master, Paddington, W., stating the date and likewise the train by which they intend to travel, and their destination in London. Parties travelling to London and desiring to engage an Omnibus, but not having previously ordered one, should request the Station Master at Swindon, Oxford or Didcot as the case may be, to telegraph to Paddington Station for an Omnibus to be in readiness, when every endeavour will be made to provide one.

The Charge for the use of an Omnibus within a 4 mile radius of Paddington Station will be ONE SHILLING PER MILE, driver and luggage included. Minimum charge THREE SHILLINGS. Sixpence per mile extra will be charged outside the radius. When the distance or the quantity of luggage is too great for one horse, and two horses become necessary, the charge for any distance will be Two Shillings per Mile, with a minimum charge of Six Shillings.

This notice is drawn from the preamble to the 1884 Great Western Railway timetable. These little buses were provided by jobmasters, although it was quite common for them to carry a railway company's name solely because they were contracted to serve their station. They had a bench for the driver and two passengers, the other six bodies facing each other in two rows of three. Their use was incredibly widespread with this GWR timetable listing at least 90 coaches, omnibuses &c., running to and from the Company's stations', including Cheddar Cliffs (all trains met), Dolgelly to Harlech, Gloucester/Ledbury, Fairford/Cirencester (2½ hour journey, later a steam 'bus), Ilfracombe/Lynton (3 hours leaving 6 pm), Llandilo/Llandovery (Sundays only) and Wantage Road via the steam tram. A footnote then reads 'Omnibuses also run to and from the Stations at the principal Towns, including Bala, Bridgnorth, Campden, Charlbury, Chipping Norton, Cleobury Mortimer, Cookham, Dolgelly, Lechlade, Llangollen, Market Drayton, Oswestry, Pangbourne, Pershore, Witney and Wrexham'.

The photograph shows Eastleigh station, London & South Western Railway, the nearest vehicle is an omnibus belonging to The George Hotel.

R.W. Kidner

An Agreement made this *seventeenth*
day of *October* 19 *03* **Between** the GREAT
CENTRAL RAILWAY COMPANY (hereinafter called "the Company")
by *Edwin Barker of Manchester*
their Agent of the one part and *The Worksop & Retford
Brewery Company L.d by Richard Henry
Allen their Secretary of Worksop
in the county of Nottingham*
(hereinafter called "the Proprietors") of the other part.

Whereas the Proprietors *have* applied to the Company for permission to
ply for hire with *two omnibuses, one four wheeled cab and two
hansom cabs* at the *Worksop* Station
of the Company, who have agreed to grant such permission, upon the terms
and conditions hereinafter appearing. **Now therefore** it is hereby mutually
agreed as follows:—

1. The Proprietors shall be at liberty to ply for hire at the said Station with
two omnibuses, one four wheeled cab & two hansom cabs

2. For such privilege the Proprietors shall pay to the Company the sum of
ten shillings & sixpence) per annum for each vehicle
commencing from the *second* day of *November 1903.*
payable *yearly in advance.*

3. The Proprietor shall comply in all respects with the regulations of the Company
in regard to the said Vehicle as detailed in the Schedule hereinafter appearing.

4. Either of the parties hereto may terminate this Agreement by giving to
the other of them Seven days' notice in writing, to expire on any day of the week,
of their or his intention to determine the same, and any notice to be served upon
the Proprietors may be either sent by post to *their* last known address,
or may be delivered to any of *their* drivers at the said Station.

5. The Proprietors shall pay the cost of stamping this Agreement.

AS WITNESS the hands of the said parties the day and year first above written.

Witness to the Signature of the said
Edwin Barker
(sgd) *J. Oldham*
G.C.R. Co Manchester   (sgd) *Edwin Barker.*
                            Agent of the Company.

Witness to the Signature of the said
Robert Henry Allen   The Worksop & Retford Brewery Co L.d
J.W. Gregory   (sgd) *Rob.t H Allen*
                            Secretary

A rare surviving document is an agreement between the Great Central Railway and the Worksop &
Retford Brewery Company allowing the latter to have available to ply for hire at Worksop station 'two
omnibuses, one four wheeled cab and two hansom cabs', each vehicle costing 2s. 6d. per annum rental.
Rules were strict including: 'The vehicle and horses shall be of a description and quality to be
approved by the Company, and each vehicle shall have rubber tyres, shall be painted in accordance
with the Company's pattern, and shall have the Company's Crest affixed on each side' and 'The first
cab or omnibus in rotation shall always have the preference if engaged for a train passenger by a
Company's servant, but the passenger shall have the option of selecting a cab or omnibus from any
part of the stand'; and fines heavy, drunkenness and insolence costing 5s. each time.

Derby's horse tram routes were opened in 1880 including a line along the London Road to Dead Man's Lane. This, unfortunately, led to Alvaston being without transport and eventually a three-horse bus was used to fill the gap being replaced by electric trams in 1904. The use of three horses indicates the terrain (and even then their life was only 2-4 years) and the waterproof covers over the 'outside' seats are an unusual touch. No uniforms were provided, of course.

A knifeboard bus c.1890. So called from the back-to-back seating upstairs. London General Omnibus Company route 'The Atlas', seemingly this worked from the Eyre Arms, St John's Wood to Bank.

Liverpool, Lord Street. Horse bus with advancing horse tram c.1900. Note the boy conductor and the precarious position of that ascending passenger. No staircase, just iron rungs, so ladies never travelled upstairs. Back-to-back seating, in bad weather it was not unknown for passengers to be thrown off as the bus lurched and drunk drivers were not entirely unknown either.

The horse as a means of motive power remained in use as a serious people-mover until at least the 1920s and in some rural parts had a revival for market day services when fuel supplies were cut 1941-1944. Although vehicles were improved from the lumbering waggons of the 17th century to the (relatively) light horse bus running in major cities until 1914, nonetheless it was a brutally hard trade for both the men involved and the animals who, in cities at least, had a short and unpleasant life. In the country, given a decent owner, horses were often cossetted rather more than the men who worked them. Modern road conditions make horse-work difficult and unfortunately we may never know whether a horse-bus made with ultra lightweight materials and modern design methods might not be one answer to moving people within ever larger pedestrian precincts; but it would be droll if the circle could be completed! This 1899 advertisement shows Threadneedle Street, London, we have evidence of the varied designs of horse buses then in service. In the centre 'outside' seating is transverse, while arriving from the right is the older, knifeboard (back-to-back) style. Other, all horse-drawn, carriages, cabs and carts complete the composition.

Stagecoach *c.*1910 but at an unknown location. Station notices read London & North Western Rly *and* Great Western Rly. The porter is cleaning a gas light but the sign only reads 'Mazawattee Tea'.

A 'genuine' but undated photograph. The destination board shows the route to have been Penge, Shortland and Beckenham. The last regular Tilling horse-drawn service ceased on 4th August, 1914. Was this one of the vehicles?

The first true horse buses were operated in London by George Shillibeer from 1829 onwards, carrying 22 passengers per trip between Paddington via Euston Road to Bank. But for some difficulties in the !ate 1830s there is a good chance buses, (Omnibuses) would now be called 'Shillies' (Shillibeers) but as he turned to running an undertaker's business the omnibus name prevailed. The second (1838) Act for regulating buses required that each driver and conductor was to wear a numbered badge for easy identification. 3861 was in use in London (MP = Metropolitan Police) between 1850 and 1902, 358 was the provincial equivalent in the 1880s and DD 83347 represents the final post-war issue.

LGOC garden seat bus *c.*1900 with transverse seating upstairs. The card is postmarked London W1 , Mar 1 12.15 pm, 1905. Re-franked St Louis, Mo. (USA) Mar 11, 5 am. All for 1*d*.

A London Omnibus

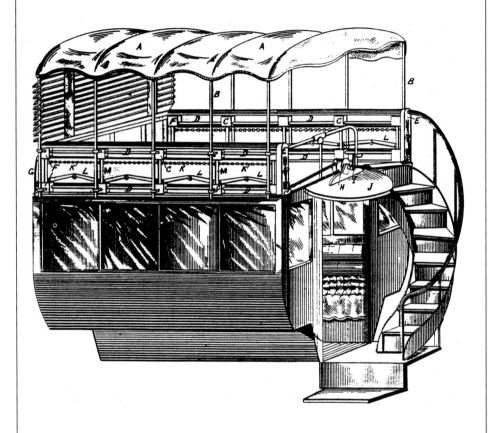

With very few exceptions (steam trams and the like) covered tops were unknown in the Victorian era. This patent, 2414 of 1889 was the result of a brainchild by two Covent Garden salesmen, Edward W.J. Hieatt and Jonathan Wash and was an 'Adjustable, Movable and Collapsible Covering for the Outsides of Omnibuses . . . and consisted of a series of hoops, covered in light tarpaulin, or other waterproof material (the number of hoops to vary according to length of Vehicle) running on two parallel bars on each side of Bus . . . The whole to be under the immediate control of one man, by means of an apparatus to which will be attached cords or wires, to draw backwards or forwards as required. The whole when not in use will remain at the head of the Vehicle'. The theory was excellent and something of the kind was tried on trams in the early years of the century and extensively found on 1920s 'Sun Saloon' coaches. In the days of horse buses the power-to-weight ratio was always a problem and when ounces (grams indeed) were being pared from bodywork the extra weight of wet canvas and iron hoops and cordage could not be countenanced.

Above: During the long reign of the horse bus many curious patents were taken out to try to improve either its manoeuvrability or weight. Obviously with a two-man crew there was a desperate need to increase the payload. This built to Hunnybun & Venden's Patent appeared in 1846, and was described as a good specimen: 'It is a tastefully and conveniently built carriage, remarkable for its low construction, thus affording easy access; so that passengers may step at once from the roadway to the floor of the carriage, without the aid of a step. The draught is considerably reduced; the peculiar, but simple construction permitting the fore-wheels to be six inches higher than usual; and the eccentric lock enabling it to turn completely in its length. The Omnibus runs particularly light, and free from noise. It is handsomely trimmed; and, both internally and exteriorly [*sic*], is a great improvement upon the usual class of omnibuses'. Imagine though, the dankness and stench inside this body with straw for the feet and no heating. Upstairs at least you were above the horse's rear and had some sort of view.

In the early days many strange methods were used to try to ensure collected fares went to the proprietor and not the conductor's tavern; Shillibeer himself found at a time when he was paying his conductors 10s. a week they boasted of pocketing £10 over and above that! The first 1*d*. tickets were issued in 1881 and covered a journey from Ludgate Circus to Charing Cross. The earliest Bell Punch machines were introduced in the London Road Car fleet during 1883, the 'General' (London General Omnibus Company) following in 1891, by which time the 1*d*. fare took one from Liverpool Street to Charing Cross. The LRC Co. ticket (*left*) is a very early one, the other anonymous issue (*right*) came from one of the constituents of the Stamford Hill consortium; each member purchasing 'Times' (i.e. 10 am, 2 pm, 5 pm departures) which he then ran on specific routes. These 'Times' were regulated by the Police to avoid excess traffic and 'fly-by-night' operators. On this ticket each 'sector' or stage (Liverpool Street/Bank or London Bridge/Elephant) represented 1*d*.'s worth of travel.

Steam Transcendent

The London and South Western Railway (later part of the Southern Railway) purchased four Clarkson steam buses in 1905 having cancelled an order for Milnes-Daimler motor buses, surely a rare victory. Two were sent to operate between Chagford and Exeter, one of which (LC 691) is seen here, but, alas, the service was only a flash-in-the-pan commencing 3rd June, 1905 and terminating 14th September, 1906, being replaced by a horse bus.

BT207, a Clarkson steam bus with Munnion (Essex) body entered service with the North Eastern Railway on 20th September, 1905. Although the Clarksons performed moderately well in cities, faced with East Coast gales the paraffin burners either blew out, or despite windshields, found the wind fanning the flames away from the 'firebox', and warming both the bodywork and the driver. After many vicissitudes the Clarksons both graduated to a shuttle service between Thirsk station and the town. Unfortunately on 7th September, 1906 the paraffin tank ignited following a blowback (although the vibration may first have loosened a fuel pipe union) and burnt out. This is what was left.

We cannot be sure whether or not this de Dion Bouton of 1898 ever ran in Britain but the artist's impression appears to be detailed enough for him to have seen the machine in the flesh even if not mobile. Curiously it has right-hand drive but details of the steering are unclear. A rather super might-have-been one fears.

Although statistics can tell lies if all the steam buses that either definitely existed or of which there is photographic evidence (but that does not mean they actually worked) are added together a total figure 300-350 does not seem unreasonable. This one is an oddity in that it was operated under special wartime licence by Newcastle Corporation during 1918. It worked almost unfailingly carrying colliers to and from the pits at Burradon to the Newcastle Corporation tram routes 19 and 20 at Four Lane Ends, Longbenton about 1½ miles away. The motive power is a Sentinel 'S' built at Shrewsbury, with a vertical boiler functioning at 230 psi - it is as well the passengers were unaware of this, but no doubt consoled themselves when they disappeared into a cloud of smoke that they were burning British coal. The whole arrangement measured roughly 24 ft long by 6 ft wide and could carry about 40 passengers.

Thornton (le) Dale lies 3 miles east of Pickering, Yorkshire and these quite remarkable photographs *c*.1905 show a pair of North Eastern Railway buses, with German-built Dürkopp 32 hp chassis and railway-built bodies. It is as well, perhaps, that the then speed limit was 12 mph; in winter these bodies were stored and coal delivery lorry bodies substituted. Buses of this type cost around £800 complete and were beyond the pockets of virtually all bar the railway companies. The lower photograph shows BT 175, the North Eastern Railway's fleet No.9, brought into service June 1905. The lettering on the chassis shows a capacity of 32; if all the faces visible travel at least 10 extra will be accommodated, testimony to the strength of the York-built body. Incidentally there were no aisles so passengers mounted by means of a ladder and one wonders how the ladies fared in their long skirts. The bodies were replaced by more orthodox designs by 1911 and, thus fitted, the Dürkopps were to survive until 1920.

Thirteen of these Belgian Germain motorbuses were purchased by the London Road Car Company in 1904/5, for whom they proved as useful as chocolate teapots. They were returned to Belgium for the fitting of more powerful engines and different gearing. The first to come back in March 1906 proved still to be incapable of climbing Notting Hill at a satisfactory speed; it and others returned were used for a time on a more level route, but after a long spell at the back of the garage some, if not all, were sold in 1908. An advertisement for the single-deck vehicle above (which actually went to Durban, South Africa) gave a cash price of £740, otherwise a deposit of £196 was required plus 12 monthly payments of £50. A top speed of 12 mph was claimed via a 4-speed gearbox with an unladen weight of 2¾ tonnes; presumably an enclosed body would add another tonne or so.

London was in many ways a honeypot for the busy bus entrepreneur and although there were many failures, mostly due to mechanical problems, nonetheless by the end of 1904 there were 31 mechanical buses in the City, and just two years later over 500 operated on 26 routes. A Scott-Stirling bus of the London Power Omnibus Company, which began running in 1902 between Kilburn and Oxford Circus, is shown.

The London & District Motor Bus Company bought three of these French Lacoste & Battman buses in 1906, shortly before the L&D was absorbed by the London Motor Bus Company.

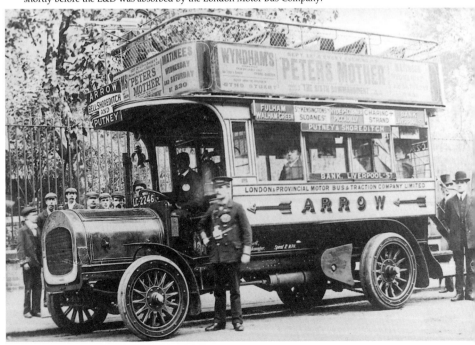

Left: At a time when almost all London buses were German or French, it was patriotic to buy a British 'National' steam bus, but although later models than this 1906 one were around until 1919, they never became widespread.

The photograph shows XU 7498, a Leyland LB5 in the fleet of 'Express', the first post-war independent to commence operations in London from 5th August, 1922, running on route 11 between Liverpool Street and Victoria. At weekends the owner of these chocolate and cream buses, A.G. Partridge, would put them in service between Hampton Court and Charing Cross. *The Omnibus Society*

The Lancashire Steam Motor Co., Ltd.

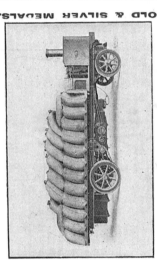

35 h.p Omnibus. 34 passengers.

5-7 Ton Steam Wagon for Municipal, General, and Colonial Service.

Write for Particulars.

Contractors to the War Office, Crown Agent for the Colonies, and many of the Largest Municipal Authorities.

Head Office and Works: LEYLAND, near PRESTON.

London Office : Cecil Chambers East, 86, Strand, W.C.

Telegrams : " Motor, Leyland." " Motatura, London."   Telephones : No. 7 Leyland 8963 Central, London,

'Over 100 repeat orders' shouts this 1907 trade press advertisement for what would become Leyland Motors. In truth, French and German chassis still dominated the London bus market; one or two 1905 Leyland buses with Crossley engines had not done well, and the half-dozen buses in the 'Kingsway' fleet were supported by Leyland, who carried out the maintenance. This operator sold out to the LGOC in 1912, who cancelled an order for 50 new Leyland buses; the 'General' had in 1909 developed its AEC X-type bus, a copy of the Leyland, and in 1910 begun making the famous B-type. However, some existing Leylands, now in 'Central' livery, were allowed to serve until 1920. Only a few years later Leyland buses were again fighting the combine, as a preferred chassis of the London 'pirates', and by 1930 the famous Leyland 'Titan' was putting 'General' buses to shame for comfort. With these still running for the 1933 London Transport, a fleet of new Leylands with SD4 diesel engines was ordered (designated STD), and in spite of all, Leyland had

Thomas Tilling Ltd was probably the largest firm of jobmasters in London. If one considers that the equivalent of every car in use today required one horse, each van two and each lorry between four and eight, all needing food, water, veterinary attention, ostlers, grooms and men who disposed of the waste product, then relief from this logistical nightmare was urgently required. They began replacing their horse bus fleet in 1911 with the TTA1 type petrol-electric bus of their own design, which gave a smoother ride; later petrol-electric models continued in service up to LPTB times.

Probably the most famous of all London bus types was 'B', with its sandwich construction chassis frame, steel wheels, worm drive and 3-speed plus reverse chain gears, 5.3 litre four-cylinder, side-valve engine developing initially about 25 hp, this rising in later models to in excess of 45 hp giving a cruising speed of 16 mph, although given a 'scorcher' of a driver this could be doubled! The whole was surmounted by a wooden-framed body initially seating 16 inside and 18 on top, the bus body being built within the legal width limit of 7 ft 2 in. Although of the latest style when first built (1910), electric lighting did not begin to supersede acetylene until 1916. The maximum number in service at any time seems to have been 2,836, although over 3,000 were built; No. 2595 LF 9592, later in service with MET (Metropolitan) and liveried accordingly.

The 1920s Learning Curve

No. 232 within the Great Western Railway's road fleet, BH 0274 was an AEC 45 hp model based on the wartime chassis powered by a Tylor engine. Registered for work on 7th November, 1919, she was originally fitted with a GWR Swindon-built char-a-banc body, but the different types of bodies were swopped about according to season and vehicular requirements. The interest here lies in the use of NAP tyres, which before reliable pneumatics were considered to give greater adhesion on cobbles and wet surfaces. The idea was that the holes (of 'scientific design') would, using Normal Air Pressure, compress slightly and squeeze the water away.

Having a Leyland SG7 chassis with Christopher Dodson 42-seat bodywork, TC 2128 was used as a demonstrator in 1923, after being ordered by Birmingham Garages Ltd at a contract price of £1,575 - a relatively high cost. This bus was sold on to United Counties for £1,400, subject to various modifications including lower ratio steering gear and a larger diameter steering wheel, this early semi-forward controlled bus, where the driver sat part way alongside the engine, proving almost impossible to handle.

The odd thing about these Bradford trolleybuses is that no matter how strange their appearance they were certainly no less odd than today's 'concept' cars - at least 581 and her sisters ran. Bradford's first service trolleys ran on 24th June, 1911, but 571 and 581 were not built until 1929, products of the English Electric works, who supplied both chassis and bodies.

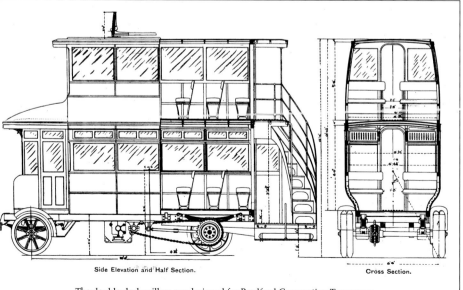

Side Elevation and Half Section.

Cross Section.

The double-deck railless car designed for Bradford Corporation Tramways.

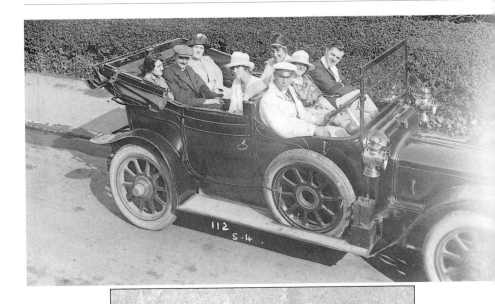

TOUR OF BOULOGNE

Daily at 2.30 p.m.

Return 6 p.m

1/6 EACH

CONDUCTED PARTIES BY

Discharged Soldier

To The

Casino

Cathedral (Crypt)

Remparts

Château (Dungeons)

War Memorial

British Cemetery

Tea at the HOTEL FRANÇOIS

Meet at the Monument in Front of Post Office

PRIVATE PARTIES SPECIALLY

ARRANGED FOR

BOULOGNE SOCIÉTÉ TYPOGRAPHIQUE

Opposite: Although no photographs appear to have survived of this operation there were a number of tours of World War I battlefields run from 1920-on, but most were short-lived and it may have been they were too soon, for, of course, travel even to France was difficult and far too expensive for most widows. We do not know the exact date of the leaflet but it was brought back by a returning officer so a guess of 1920-1922 would seem reasonable. The tram ticket *(above)* is of the same date and both items are remarkable survivals. The type of vehicle the 'discharged soldier' would have used would be similar to this which, passed down from a Ducal family, found itself on trip work. Spare (pneumatic tyred) wheel, accumulators, carbide lamps and outside handbrake make a pleasantly period scene.

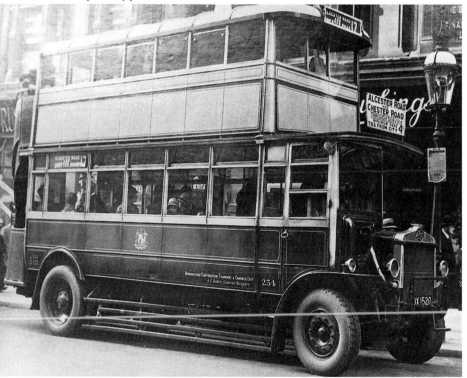

In the early days of buses bodywork did not necessarily come from one of the 'mass' manufacturers but at least until the 1930s could be quite homespun - perhaps purchased from a local car bodybuilder because he happened to be married to the niece of the boss. This could, and often did, go wrong with height/width/length/weight not meeting legal requirements; even if it was ever completed. The body might leak, sag, prove to have windows held in with putty (surprisingly often this!), seats held by coachbolts, or a boot floor that spread when in use. As late as 1947 Jim Batty, an operator within the Wansbeck Valley, purchased a Commer Q4 new (CNL 592) and had it bodied locally. 'It was the first bus-body the builder had ever tried and gave more and more trouble until, a mere five years later, it disintegrated'. OX 1520 *(above)*, a 1927 ADC 507 with Short Bros of Rochester bodywork must have been quite a familiar apparition to tram passengers in Birmingham as the similarities in the external design could have been deliberate. Route 17 Alcester Road to Chester Road was a through, express route carrying the high minimum fare of 4*d*., when trams still had 1*d*. stages. It was withdrawn in 1935.

Cross Roads. Layer-De-La-Haye. 123370

Assuming this photograph dates back to the late 1920s Layer de la Haye, Essex, had a population of about 650, and this little bus was perfectly adequate for the 3½ mile journey to Colchester, the market town. There are three ladies (all with hats) on board, and although we do not know who built the bus it fits absolutely wonderfully into the somnolent

Treble Acting
Emergency Door Rim Lock.
GABRIEL'S PATENT.

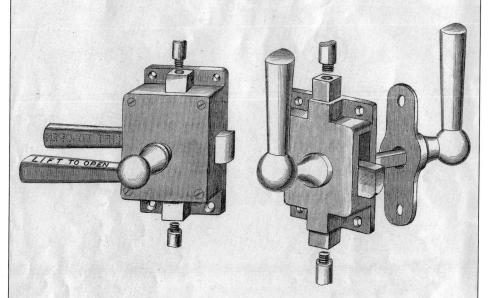

No. 5326   No. 5423.

This Rim Lock is specially designed for the Emergency Doors of Motor Buses, and is fitted inside the Vehicle. It has 3 Locking Bolts, Top, Bottom and Side and is fitted with Interior and Exterior Handles and is so arranged that by operating either of these all three bolts are simultaneously withdrawn. No. 5326 is arranged as a Slam Lock, and in our No. 5423 the side bolt folds inwards. The Top and Bottom Bolts are supplied in steel, and are screwed into the top and bottom of locks and are provided with the necessary staples in which these bolts work. It is absolutely a Safety Lock, and entirely prevents any rattling of the door when in service. It has no complicated parts and is Dust Proof, and complies with the requirements of the leading Licensing Authorities.

Price ... ... **23/6** each, complete with Handles.
Lighter Pattern, **17/6** „ „ „ „

Patentees and Sole Manufacturers:
GABRIEL & CO., 4 & 5, A. B. ROW, BIRMINGHAM.

When the new motor omnibuses began to take the shapes recognisable today, this advancement also led to certain legal requirements being stipulated by local licensing authorities; usually the Police or Watch Committee. Clearly on a char-a-banc with perhaps 10 doors and no roof in the event of a rough shunt the way out was obvious, but not so on a semi-enclosed single decker. Every brassfounder in the country hastened to help manufacturers meet the new requirements.

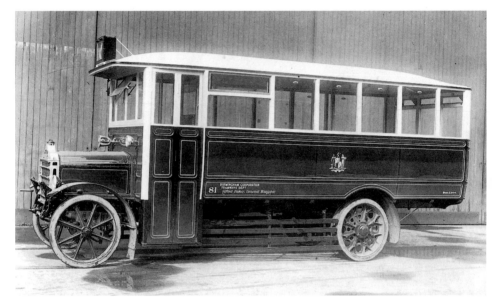

No. 81 with the Birmingham fleet had a Daimler CK2 chassis and a local-built Buckingham body delivered in 1923, and withdrawn 1931. The sheer beauty of the lining out and the neatness of the whole design gave OL 1714 a distinctive charm. Of the Leyland (*below*) we are only certain it is a 1922 'A' type, probably a demonstrator and said, once again, to have a Buckingham body. Again, this is a fine example of bodybuilders' and coachpainters' art.

FN 5052, a 1921 Tilling-Stevens TS3AX char-a-banc caught fire one August when three years old on the road from Folkestone. Traditional firemen with their brass helmets (abandoned later due to the risk of falling overhead power lines) and fire-axes are damping down the wreckage. No attempt was made to repair the machine and it was scrapped. *M&D and East Kent Bus Club*

The vehicles belonging to some operators tended to look gnarled long before they were scrapped. In some cases this was due to an archaic form of bodywork while in others neglect took its toll. It is difficult to envisage that this Darlington Triumph Services 1929 Leyland Lion was painted deep scarlet with black and yellow lining, the upperworks being cream, but it was so. Unfortunately she was really too long-lived and, although reduced to the status of 'spare' or 'duplicate' bus (as here at Barnard Castle) could not be called much of an advertisement for the company when withdrawn in 1949.

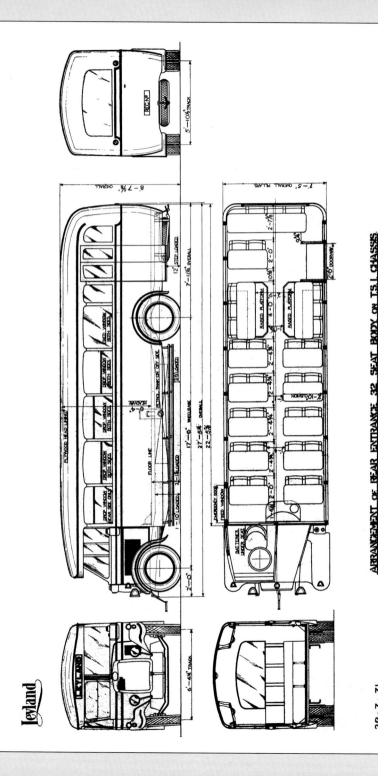

ARRANGEMENT OF REAR ENTRANCE 32 SEAT BODY ON T.S.I. CHASSIS.

Leyland

28 - 7 - 31

The period between the late 1920s and the 1930s saw massive development of chassis, engines and to some degree, bodywork by the larger concerns, who by virtue of their sales (even in times of depression) could keep research staff at work. The Leyland TS1 'Tiger' chassis and their appropriate in-house bodywork first appeared on the market in 1927, powered by a six-cylinder 6.79 litre petrol engine with a sliding mesh gearbox. The vehicle was relatively fast (although the maximum permitted speed was only 20 mph), the engine developing 105 hp at 2,000 rpm. The wooden-framed body style was typical of the time and the infamous offset driver's seat remained even in the 1931 variant.

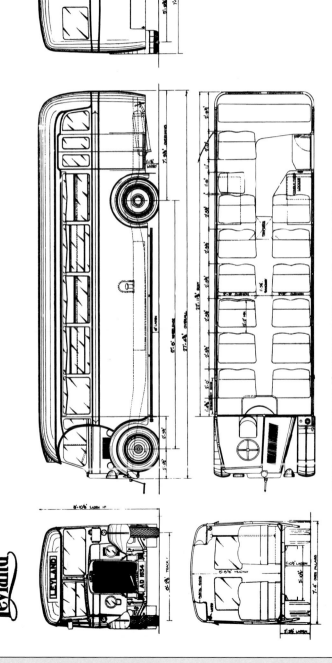

ARRANGEMENT OF STANDARD 32 SEATER REAR ENTRANCE BODY ON TS6 CHASSIS

17-10-33

The TS6 appeared just one year (1933) after the TS1 was withdrawn, but now Leyland offered either a 7.59 litre petrol engine or the new and powerful 8.6 diesel driving through a modernized gearbox. Bodywork was by now steel-framed and the driver's non-adjustable seat at long last was square to the steering wheel, and it is of note that, by contrast with the 7 year life of wooden-framed buses, some TS6 Tigers kept their original bodywork into the early 1950s.

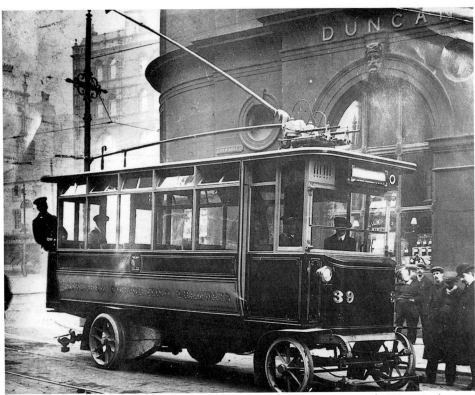

At one time or another from 1911 onwards in excess of 5,000 trolleybuses were in use in the UK, ranging from the 1,800 or so of London to the two of Dundee. The old name of 'railless tramcar' almost sums them up as they were electrically propelled with one or more motors driving the rear wheels. Early models had independent motors driving each wheel, including in 1901 a four-wheel-drive model, while for some years a hand operated tramcar-like controller regulated the speed; the driver also having to steer and use the handbrake! The next four photographs show some of the variety in use before World War I. Rotherham's first cars entered service on 3rd October, 1912, No. 39 is a chain-driven Straker, here having one boom down and earthing itself through the tramrail – in effect a steerable tram, whereas the winter scene shows the work they had, tiny solid-tyred wheels notwithstanding.

Above: Keighley began 2nd May, 1913 using a remarkable system patented by Mercedes Stoll. The motors were built into the rear wheels with electric brakes and the current collection was 'interesting' as no booms were utilized, but instead a 28 lb. trolley ran between the wires. This gadget had four wheels and a plumb-bob weight to keep it *in situ* and it was connected to the bus via a spring loaded cable about 25 ft long. When a car met another as staged here, they both stopped and swopped power cables, there being only one set of wires.

Left: The Mexborough & Swinton system owed its existence to two main factors - the original tramway used a quite unreliable contact stud system (Dolter) and mining-induced subsidence. The railless routes (3¾ miles) opened in the turmoil of war, 31st August, 1915. The chassis and bodywork of No. 47 was of an almost forgotten make (Garrett of Leiston, Suffolk), delivered 1928.

The next four photographs tell a tale of labour's lost. Karriers were built in Huddersfield by a firm founded in 1907 and whose greatest days were during World War I when they produced over 2,000 4 ton lorries. After 1919 they returned to building buses and coaches of no great distinction but little worse than their contempories. Logically, and having an eye to the rates, Huddersfield Corporation Tramways supported local industry, but by 1934 the goodwill of the company passed to the Rootes Group, largely as Karrier seemed to have had a penchant for getting small details wrong, like choosing a particularly horrible engine, the Dorman 6 JUL - awkward in boats it was impossible in a bus. On 22nd April, 1922 services commenced between Honley, New Mill and Jackson Bridge. This is the opening scene at the Jackson Bridge Terminus, the buildings were still there in 1996. The first bus is a Guy BA, the second a Karrier.

This shows the opening of the Honley-Holmfirth-Holmbridge service on 15th April, 1922. The view is in Huddersfield Road, Holmfirth in front of what is now the Library and Postcard Museum.

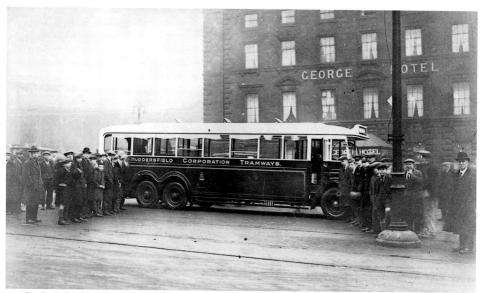

Single-decker No. 60 outside the still extant George Hotel. The reason for the photograph was to 'show off' the new bus as Huddersfield always liked to make a practice of showing off their newest acquisitions to the public in St George's Square. It seems to have started in December 1909 when trams 71 to 75 arrived newly-built from UEC and one of them was paraded in the square prior to entering service. Karrier WL6 with NCME 36-seat bodywork and a 4 mpg taste for petrol - on the flat!

The parade of single-deckers is taken in front of Huddersfield station which from its inception has always had a large open area in front. On 16th May, 1930 the motor buses were transferred from Huddersfield Corporation Tramways to the Huddersfield Joint Omnibus Committee (a partnership between Huddersfield Corporation and the LMS Railway Co.). This area has been available to pedestrians long before the word 'pedestrianisation' was ever thought of!

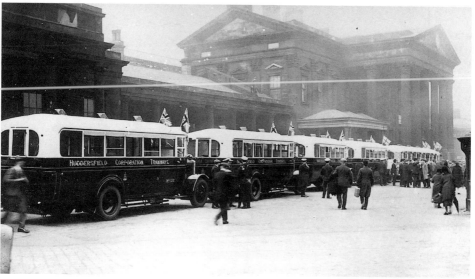

Antique to look at even in the 1920s, nonetheless the buses served to bring Market Day passengers into Bury St Edmunds, 1920s.
J. Neale

This view is chosen to remind us all of the unsophisticated travel enjoyed in the inter-war years. Few people had cars of any shape and those that did were unlikely to want to travel with 20 or 30 strangers on a day out to anywhere. Perhaps the passengers shown would not have had electricity - gas lighting still being the norm, and probably no more than 50 per cent would have access to flushing toilets. Even in the 1950s this applied, it was odd to live in a cottage with well water and paraffin lighting and to park a modern-ish coach outside! This view is at Deal in Kent. The char-a-banc has solid front tyres, with pneumatic rear ones.

Who pays for the provision of bus shelters and the facilities offered has long been a bone of contention between councils and operators. If the council supply reasonable amenities then they expect operators to pay a rent for the use of their bus stands. If operators pay for the building or shelter, reasonably, they expect sole use. Passengers want facilities provided, do not want to pay and, alas, all too often wreck whatever provision is made. In this view we see sunshine at Bovey station (Devon), *c.*1923.

Summertime, Maidstone, 1922.

M&D and East Kent Bus Club

Although this couple of photographs are of different operators' vehicles they make an interesting pair. Since trams arrived on the scene with almost invariably open top decks, inventors vexed their minds trying to find ways of keeping the seats dry. Both tram and bus passengers would, not unnaturally, prefer to crowd in downstairs than be cold and wet upstairs. Both are Short Bros bodies on Leyland chassis but with detail differences in their seating and hence means of attachment for the tarpaulins.

These two photographs, drawn from the collection of the M&D and East Kent Bus Club, show the contrast between 1928 and 1953 bus interiors. The top photograph depicts a Leyland TD1 with a Short Bros of Rochester 48-seat body, having an open platform, open staircase and open top. The more modern illustration below is of a 1953 Park Royal-bodied Guy Arab IV. Not only is the back enclosed but there is a heater!

The very concept of the Tilling-Stevens bus sounds particularly archaic today. The principle was simple with a (petrol) engine driving a compound-wound generator which in turn drove through a speed controller and reversing switch to a series - wound electric motor coupled directly to the cardan-shaft and so to the back axle. It was heavy, relatively slow in acceleration and eventually proved to be incapable of enlargement beyond a moderate size. But, bear in mind that gearboxes were pretty dreadful to handle without crashing and clashing before the late 1920s, that horses were still the norm and finally most drivers learned to drive on tramcars. Given that any gearless motor will always be smoother than driving via a 'crash' gearbox and given the type of drivers available, the Tilling-Stevens was an operator's dream. The first diagram from a 1929 booklet shows the steady increase in torque available, the second how improvements had been made in petrol-electric bus acceleration, and the third, tested on the precursor of today's tachograph, shows the quite remarkable differences that existed in passenger ride comfort. This bus is Maidstone & District fleet No. 77, KL 9004, a TS6 delivered in August 1925 with a Short Bros body and photographed in 1931.

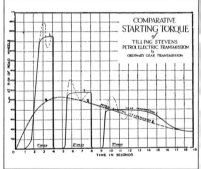

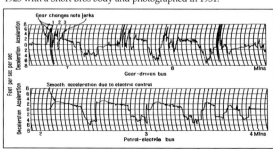

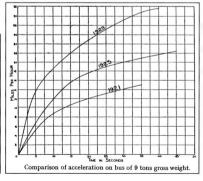

Comparison of acceleration on bus of 9 tons gross weight.

'Trip char-a-banc gangwayed' was the official name, but first you see them and then you don't! Although these photographs are clearly staged, is it intriguing to see just how a standard bus used for outings could metamorphose into an enclosed model given inclement weather. That said and done our relatives have stated that in the 1920s it was easier to get wet than for the driver and male passengers to spend 20 minutes erecting the roof and assembling the side sheets (if they had not got left behind anyway!). That 20 minutes was another 10 miles nearer the destination. The alternative was for the driver to stop at a hostelry, and for the passengers to disembark while he put up the wet-weather gear. FN 7451 was one of a batch of 12 Tilling-Stevens B9A with Tilling bodywork carrying 31 'charabanc', seats, delivered in 1926. After being down-seated to 26 in 1932 this bus was rebodied with a redundant 1928 Brush saloon in 1934, and finally withdrawn two years later.

The M&D and East Kent Bus Club

During the inter-war period many smaller coach operators sought niche markets and, alas, all too often wandered up blind alleys. As yet unregistered this Strachans-bodied (Associated Daimler) ADC was limited to 20 mph and had a very short life as a coach.

The Albatross postcard highlights all too clearly the main problem inherent in the interior design. For reasons of weight and safety no rigid intermediate doors could be fitted between the cabins and whatever the nominal privacy offered by curtains, the enforced proximity of other bodies (who might be snoring, drunk or just unhygienic) was to be their Achilles' heel.

Interior View, looking forward.   ALBATROSS ROADWAYS LTD.

A depot view taken during the transition period between tram and bus operations of the Wakefield & District Light Railway Company, and their bus-owning subsidiary, the West Riding Automobile Co. Ltd. This is the Belle Isle repair shop, Wakefield, where tram maintenance was similar to railway work with extensive engineering equipment being required. Buses, by contrast, are quite flimsy and 'tishy'.

A myth has grown up that London was always full of boring old red buses all as alike as peas in a pod. At no time was this entirely true as even in the dullest era, that of the Routemaster, this class contained a number of variants. During the early 1930s, the heyday of the independents, although the outline of the vehicles was standardized by the actions of the Police Commissioner, the names of the operators and their liveries were quite exciting. Later, after the war, a keen bus-spotter could find incredible variety among the visible vehicles with at least half-a-dozen different paint styles in central London alone. The view above shows Chariot AEC Regent GJ 8501.

The Omnibus Society

A.G. Summerskill Leyland TD1 GC 5781   *R.W. Kidner*

Renown Leyland TD1.   *The Omnibus Society*

Express Leyland TD1 UW 8157 (contrast with XU 7498 on page 25).   *The Omnibus Society*

SOUTHERN RAILWAY

RAIL AND ROAD TOURS!

CHEAP RETURN TICKETS

in conjunction with

DEVON GENERAL OMNIBUS COMPANY, LTD.

will be issued

DAILY, JULY 6th, and until further notice

available by all Trains and Road Motors from 8.0 a.m., as under:—

From EXETER (Queen Street)

	3rd Class by Rail. s. d.
TO	
BUDLEIGH SALTERTON	2/-
OKEHAMPTON	3/3
SIDMOUTH	2/7

AND VICE VERSA.

Passengers journey forward by rail for return by any Devon General Road Motor the same day, or vice versa.

New Combined Day Fares to Orcombe Point, via Exmouth

(JULY to SEPTEMBER 21st, inclusive).

FROM	DEPART		RETURN FARES. 3rd Class by Rail.
	Weekdays.	Sundays.	s. d.
EXETER (Queen Street) ...	All Trains 8.15 a.m. to 5.38 p.m.	All Trains 8.50 a.m. to 7.20 p.m.	1/9
	6.5, 6.42 and 7.23 p.m. ...	—	1/1
POLSLOE BRIDGE HALT	All Trains 8.22 a.m. to 5.45 p.m.	All Trains 8.55 a.m. to 7.27 p.m.	1/7
	6.47, 7.28 p.m.		1/1
TOPSHAM	All Trains 8.30 a.m. to 7.37 p.m.	All Trains 9.4 a.m. to 7.38 p.m.	1/-

Tickets available by any Devon General Omnibus from Exmouth to Orcombe Point and vice versa or for throughout return by Road to either Topsham or Exeter (Paul Street Bus Station).

CONDITIONS UPON WHICH THESE CHEAP TICKETS ARE ISSUED.

These tickets are issued subject to the conditions published in the Company's Time Tables and Notices and in the Railway Companies " Book of Regulations relating to Traffic by Passenger Train or other similar service " and to the following special conditions :—

(i) Neither the holder nor any other person shall have any right of action against the Company or any other Company or person owning, working or using any railway, vehicles, vessels or premises (whether jointly with the Company or otherwise) upon which such tickets may be available in respect of (a) injury (fatal or otherwise), loss, damage or delay, however caused, or (b) loss of or damage or delay to property, however caused.

(ii) The tickets are not transferable ; they are available only by the trains and on the days specified in the Company's Notices and (except where otherwise permitted by the Company's regulations) from and to the stations named on the tickets.

(iii) Children under three years of age free when accompanied by a fare-paying passenger ; children of three years of age and under 14 years of age half-fares.

(iv) No luggage allowed except small handbags, luncheon baskets or other small articles intended for the passenger's personal use.

Waterloo Station, S.E. 1,

July, 1930.

H. A. WALKER,
General Manager.

C.X. 2634/ 10/2730.

* Waterlow & Sons Limited, London, Dunstable & Watford.

Combined road and rail trips were, and indeed are, quite extensively offered almost since the beginning of reliable rail travel, with horse-drawn waggonettes conveying passengers between railheads along a scenic route, the whole journey being covered by an inclusive fare. This Southern Railway leaflet of 1930 offers a number of permutations for a pleasant day out by rail and coach.

Above: The bus is LT1 Leyland with a Hall Lewis body delivered 1930 and is seen at Abbey Place, Torquay, when quite new. Although here on route 1 Torquay to Exeter, together with driver Les Dolvear, all 10 of this class regularly worked to Orcombe Point.
L.F. Folkard

Left: Devon General bus tickets required two punches, the upper for the date and the lower for the fare stage; conductors, especially on summer reliefs, needed to be extremely dextrous given that holiday passengers rarely know where they are going and never have the right change.
R.W. Kidner

Below: The locomotive and its train are waiting in 1929 at Sidmouth on the local service for which these Adams class '02' 0-4-4T engines were well suited.
G. Beckett

The great majority of small tramway networks became effectively life expired during the 1930s when their trackwork and cars alike required replacement. Given the slump conditions prevailing there was little enough money around for basic services, let alone expecting the hard-pressed ratepayers to pay for what was perceived to be an outmoded form of transport. So off with the old and on with the new, in this case Wallasey Corporation whose trams were phased out gradually,. the last line expiring 30th November, 1933. Like many other operators, Wallasey suffered from a desire to experiment with different chassis builders' products, and furthermore their General Manager designed a unique twin staircase arrangement for their bodies which incorporated a rear entrance/front exit layout - this as long ago as 1931. However, this photograph also is not all it seems for these vehicles Nos.75-85 were photographed at the bodybuilders, English Electric, and so smitten by this were the Daimler Company that they used it in their rather beautiful 1934 handbook showing examples of vehicles recently delivered. Fine in a way but only the front 5 are of Daimler manufacture, with material differences (chrome wheel nut guards on the rear vehicles and differing hubs among other items) marking out the 6 Leyland TD2s behind. The Daimler were a less common model, the CP6, having six-cylinder poppet valve (petrol) engines, perhaps slightly underpowered at 6,561 cc. They were sold to Kingston-upon-Hull Corporation in 1941.

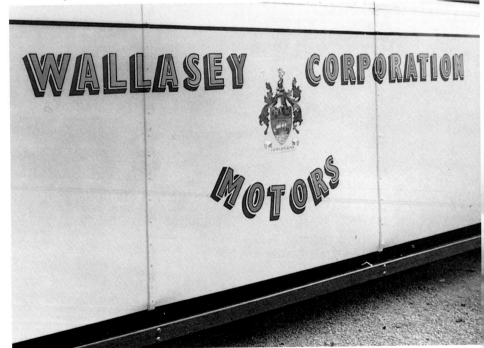

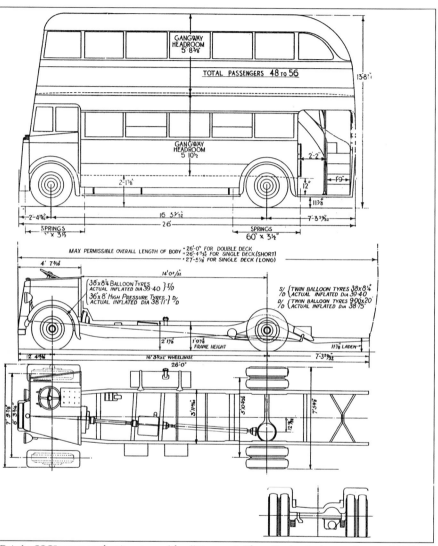

The Daimler COG5 passenger chassis was one of the all-time greats. The coding breaks down as Commercial Oil Gardner 5-cylinder (type 5LW, a Light Weight derivative of Gardner's marine, oil engine). In its day the combination of this reliable, unburstable, diesel, an almost indestructible chassis, 10 mpg against 6 mpg for a petrol-engined equivalent and particularly a fluid fly-wheel together with five-speed pre-select gearbox, had its sales only hampered by a slightly higher than average price (chassis alone £1,575 against Leyland's £1,450) and, from time to time, a relatively long delivery time. Within the parameters of its day, 60-odd years ago, the acceleration figures for this 10 ton bus were excellent, particularly given that the gear changes were jerk-free when many drivers were faced with fairly dreadful crash gearboxes. The recorded top speed (37 mph) was perfectly acceptable for city work. Braking efficiency, which was tested very thoroughly with a simulated full load of passengers, was more than adequate; especially as air-braked equivalents (and the COG5 was still available until the 1960s) could be too fierce for passengers' ease-of-mind when driven by a motorised 'Erbert. A reviewer in 1934 summed up this typical British double-deck bus thus: 'Altogether then, this Daimler is a vehicle of which the maker may justly be proud. It is beautifully finished and of thoroughly modern design . . .'

Stockton Corporation purchased Leyland vehicles prior to 1930/31, when the General Manager ordered a fleet of comparative vehicles for tram replacement service. Leyland, Bristol, AEC, Crossley and Daimler chassis, bodies came from Leyland, Bristol, Brush, Park Royal, Short Bros and Crossley, finalising in the choice of Daimler CP6 chassis incorporating poppet valve petrol engines, batches being ordered in 1932 and 1934. By this time the Gardner diesel-engined COG 5 chassis had come on stream, this then being the preferred machine, albeit with Cravens of Sheffield bodywork. No. 15 was one of three delivered in 1936, surviving with Stockton until 1949. A particular note on the bodywork relates to the General Manager's choice of straight staircases; unlike most bodies these did not face the passenger entry but lay at right angles to the platform. Seating was reduced by one to 26 on each deck. The semi-streamlined paintwork style was in vogue in the 1930s; this was more elegant than most

Thornycroft have been described as having been in the second division of bus chassis manufacturers. Their main income was always from the marine side of their business with lorries second and PSVs a rather unfortunate long way behind. Typically in 1925 an operator could buy a fully reconditioned ex-WD J-type bus chassis with six months' guarantee for £300, when the factory wanted £900 for a similar machine with no guarantee. The chassis under this body is an LC-DD, one of four bought by Cardiff Corporation in 1930, designed for single deck bodywork and fitted with puny 4-cylinder 35 hp engines. This may have been a special cut price job (they cost £765 complete), and it is known that four 'stock' bodies were obtained from Hall Lewis in April 1930 at £500 each in lieu of the normal £700. The design was relatively 'old hat', but Hall Lewis (a firm with Welsh origins) were to be dragged down by the failure of a colliery, selling out and reforming as Park Royal Vehicles. The brakes on this quartet were tishy, requiring adjustment several times a day and relining twice a week. In 1934 Gardner 6 LW diesel engines were somehow fitted by Watts of Lydney at £535 each. Although far heavier these could be used to assist the 'stopability' of these pathetic machines, and gave an economy of 10 mpg in lieu of the 3 mpg of the petrol burners. The quartet were withdrawn in early 1943, Cardiff advertising BC and LC-type chassis spares a year later, the vehicles themselves either being scrapped or sold to showmen albeit the Gardner engines were refitted into Crossley chassis then on order.

A magnificent example of an indiginous bus is seen at the Mare Street triangle, Hackney, East London, looking from Westgate Street on 13th December, 1938. GO 7200 had an AEC Renown chassis with a Chiswick-built body seating 35 and the cinema via route 236 was showing Edward G. Robinson in 'Passport to Fame'.

Some bus workings were fearsome and none worse than Bargoed Hill, where vehicles operated by the West Monmouthshire Omnibus Board routinely trundled up and down. Conditions were so bad that this ostensibly normal vehicle had a lorry (Leyland Beaver) chassis fitted with a sprag which dug in the road should it run back and the handbrake operated on all four wheels. Entering service in 1935 AAX 27 was numbered 13 in the fleet and against all odds survived not only until 1959 in service, but the chassis was later preserved.

Omnibus Society

The bodywork on this Maudslay ML7 for Coventry Corporation was built by the Brush Electrical Engineering Company of Loughborough to a particularly archaic design. The front upstairs emergency window is particularly of note. Seating 50, VC 9667 was the last of a batch of 4 and after passing this stability test of 28° was delivered in October 1931. Although sold off by the corporation in 1939, it is known No. 58 saw further service in the London area.

This drawing is from a mid-1920s Maudslay catalogue and shows a low-line model double-deck bus of the period. Mechanically this bus has a 4-cyl. petrol engine developing 36 hp. Curiosities (by modern standards) include the angled downstairs seating and the complex staircase. The braking system was interesting: 'Brakes on all four road-wheels, 18 in. dia. drums at front, 24 in. dia. at rear. There is also a foot-operated transmission-brake. Those on the front wheels are servo-operated, working through the medium of the foot-brake. The rear-wheel brakes are hand-controlled, and each set is perfectly balanced. All shoes are cam-operated, friction-faced, and expand inside the steel drums. There are ready means for adjustment', and the clutch 'inverted cone, leather-to-metal engagement' was short-lived. However, the most archaic note to modern ears lay in the driving controls: 'H.T. magneto having differentiated coupling to give fine adjustment. Spark and throttle controlled by friction-faced finger-levers neatly located above the steering wheel. The usual form of independent foot-accelerator is fitted'.

MAUDSLAY
REG'D

General Outline and Seating Plans of Maudslay Low-Level Safety Omnibuses.

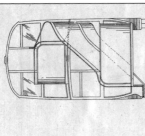

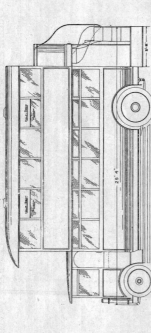

Maudslay Covered-in Low-Level Omnibus with 54 seats.

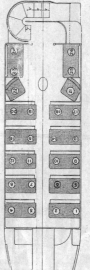

Lower Seating Plan, Double-Deck Omnibus.

Top Seating Plan, Double-Deck Omnibus.

Maudslay 35-Seater Single-Deck Low-Level Omnibus.

Seating Plan, Single-Deck Omnibus.

This Park Royal 'all metal'-bodied AEC Regent entered service with Morecambe & Heysham in 1938, after being an exhibit at the 1937 Commercial Motor Show. No. 45, CTF 861, survived over 20 years, by which time she was one of the last petrol-engined double-deckers in Britain, quite fitting the 'genteel' image of Morecambe with their quiet running and silent tickover. The lump by the bulkhead was the Autovac which was designed to overcome the problem of getting petrol from a low level tank to a high level carburettor without resource to a then unreliable petrol pump or worse on a PSV, a pressurised system. Instead the Autovac relies on a vacuum chamber to suck the fuel to the header tank. The feed is via a watchmaker's paradise of check valves and it was not unknown on long uphill stretches for the pump to act exactly as vacuum-operated windscreen wipers and run out of suck-em. Morecambe buses only ran on the level. However, having said that, Autovacs used sensibly were (and are) a very quiet method for progressing fuel – today's demand for spares comes not only from PSV owners but those who have Rolls-Royce and Bentley cars. No. 45 was, it seems, the only bus in the fleet to carry this 'streamlined' livery (in vogue elsewhere in the late 1930s) but the 'Sunsaloon' folding roof required a very upright rear profile.

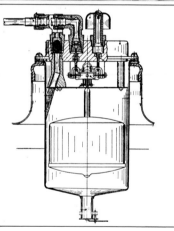

e 'Sunsaloon Head' roll-over fabric roof (not similar to that used on the Citroen 2CV) racted into a container at the rear, 1 in the event of rain the bus iductor or coach driver was ected to wind it forward. ile the roof worked well ugh the inherent weakness the body led to most being elled over in later years. other not dissimilar design s the 'Walman', used by Short s in their bodies for Southdown. .931 description explains the method working: 'Briefly, the action of the hood ends on endless roller chains worked by a handle. hoodsticks, instead, however, of being attached direct to the chains are connected by flat metal stays or links lyingly flat and parallel with the chains when the hood is fully extended, and folding up with the hood when the latter is open'. Initially an opening of 15 ft x 4 ft was achieved but this was reduced on later batches. An alternative form of opening roof were the 'Davidson' sliding hatches which 'are ideally suited for the roofs of double-deckers. Being rigid, the hatches can be made quite watertight, and they are very easy to open or close, whilst there seemed no reason why they should rattle'. The 1929 illustration shows a 'Sunsaloon Head', albeit on a single-decker.

No. 493 of the Birmingham Corporation Tramway & Omnibus Department was built in 1931 with an AEC Regent chassis and a Metro-Cammell Saltley-assembled body seating 48. Although withdrawn in 1945, prior to this 493 was to see service with London Transport. The BCT fleet was as up-to-date as could be with these Regents, proof lying in the

The Morris Commercial Imperial was not the most successful of chassis types, only 83 being manufactured. No. 504 in the Birmingham Corporation bus fleet (OC 504) was delivered in 1934 with Brush of Loughborough 51-seat bodywork, as one of four designs, the other three coming from English Electric, Gloucester Railway Carriage & Wagon and Metro-Cammell, although Metro-Cammell was eventually to body the majority of this tranche of chassis (Nos. 507-53). Rather surprisingly 504 was not withdrawn until 1942, by which time she was very non-standard and spares were impossible to obtain.

Very obviously posed to show its low height this Hall Lewis-bodied AEC Regent demonstrator was deliberately painted in Glasgow Corporation yellow, orange and green (albeit with non-standard silver roof) in the hope of winning orders, although the low capacity (50 seat) body arrangement forced on Hall Lewis by their patented upstairs arrangement of twin sunken gangways and central seats was not acceptable to Glasgow. In any event this body manufacturer became bankrupt just nine months after this photograph was taken in July 1929 but reformed as Park Royal Vehicles shortly afterwards. An interesting note is the provision of a spare wheel. Eventually this machine became an AEC staff 'hack' conveying workmen.

Low bridges forced most operators into buying vehicles that were really most difficult and unsatisfactory to work. With the conductor's revenue collection hardly enhanced by his not having extendable arms for the four-in-a-row upstairs seats, and many a passenger aggravated by banging their heads on the low ceiling beneath the trough when sitting downstairs, the arrival of the Bristol Lodekka with its offset shaft was more than welcome. Typical of 'traditional' vehicles, although only seating 24 passengers on each deck, Weymann was forced into seeking an ingenious solution just to get these in on a Bristol G05G chassis in 1936 (*this page*), while Park Royal managed 53 (26 upstairs), albeit in some discomfort, in its 1936 body on a Leyland TD4 chassis (*opposite*).

(All) M&D and East Kent Bus Club

Rather unfortunately there has grown up a myth that the best bus days were in the 1930s. The reality was that the big railway-owned companies either bought up the independents, ran them into the ground or just waited for both the men and their routes to fall like ripe plums when their original vehicles either wore out or they found the hire purchase payments too onerous. In 1927 around 40 companies or individuals ran buses through Ilkeston, Derbyshire, on more or less regular services. By 1937 just 10 remained and four died fairly quickly thereafter; Royal Blue (1941), Excelsior (1937) and Winfield Star (1940) to Barton Transport, while Midland General collected Heanor & District in 1938. Today's deregulation is merely an example of history repeating itself. Here we see the fast bus of H. Boxall of the type which could outrun almost any of the 'Big Companies' vehicles, but note the use of a boy conductor and lack of uniforms.

In many ways this green Chevrolet with its locally-built bodywork typified the light fast buses of the late 1920s and early 1930s. E. & H. Frakes were the operators, but having spent their original cash on a pair of buses when renewal time came earnings had slumped and there was no choice other than to sell out to a big company.

If the driver of this Western National 1929 Leyland Titan running between Plymouth and Tavistock had an accident, regardless of cause, he was immediately suspended without pay pending an enquiry. If the conductor made a loss in change or collected counterfeit money his wages were docked the amount. Were they really 'good old days'?

This Burnley 1930 Leyland LT2, sitting at Queensgate Garage, has had a puncture, and indeed until the early 1960s such an occurrence, if not commonplace, was far from unusual. One day a coach driver panted his way into the local garage rolling a large heavy wheel. 'Have you got an air line, mate?', he enquired of the attendant. Without looking up that individual replied, 'No, but we have three buses a day'. Seriously, the size and weight of a PSV wheel has to be experienced and one dropped can break a leg too easily - and it is nearly always the inside rear that gets punctured.

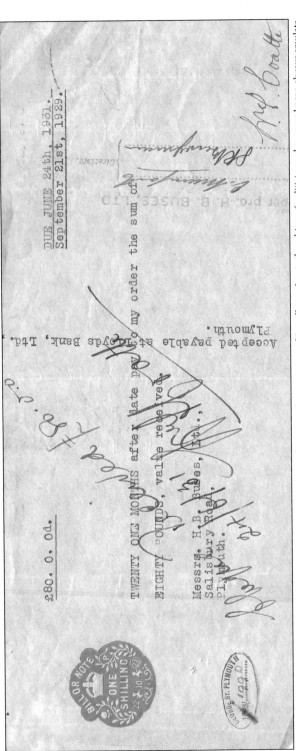

DUE JUNE 24th, 1931.

September 21st, 1929.

£80. 0. 0d.

TWENTY ONE MONTHS after date pay to my order the sum of

EIGHTY POUNDS, value received.

Messrs. H.B. Buses, Ltd.,
Salisbury Road,
Plymouth.

Accepted payable at Lloyds Bank, Ltd.,
Plymouth.

per pro. H. B. BUSES LTD

Directors

BILL OR NOTE
ONE SHILLING

The whole subject of vehicle licensing has always been complex and for the average bus operator, subject all too often to the whims of politicians who, as we know, always emulate Nanny in believing they alone know what is good for us. Early operators tended to have started with a convertible vehicle only later really organising their bus work to a timetable under pressure from rival companies. Very, very many went under. If one had cash to invest later then the simplest procedure was to buy up a company garage, route and staff. Technically, it was of dubious legality to buy or sell a route as it could be withdrawn by the Traffic Commissioner and, of course, what is goodwill? No route, no goodwill. However this rare survivor shows it could and did happen. This promissory note was given by H.B. Buses of Plymouth for payment to Mr Coath of Eddystone Motors (also of Plymouth) whose bus service 'H.B.' acquired. Signed, Clarence Mumford and J.R. Berryman, Directors of 'H.B.'.

Three Morris Commercial Viceroys of 1931 (and that was a rare enough chassis) are seen outside the Harrington Coach Works at Hove when absolutely new. Their neat 20-seat 'Allweather' bodies were ideal for countryside tours and, as 20-seaters, they were not required to carry conductors if used for bus work. All were requisitioned by the Ministry of War Transport in July 1940, but one or more survived another seven years.

M&D and East Kent Bus Club

As buses get older, even when they survive, it is a precarious life being at the whim of the garage foreman or his senior officers. If space is short out they go, but if not then nowadays preservation may be possible. Seen here at Douglas, Isle of Man, are, left to right, MN 5105 (ex-Manxland Bus Services in 1929) as Isle of Man Road Services No. 49, a Leyland PLSCI Lion with Massey 28-seat bodywork, new 1927, withdrawn 1951, and JMN 455 (ex-KVT 284 on the mainland) No. 87 in the IOMRS fleet, a 1947 Commer Commando with a 32-seat Waveney body, after 1967 a henhouse! Finally, the double-decker is KMN 517, No. 9 in the fleet, a fairly standard Leyland PD2/1 with Leyland 56-seat bodywork new in 1949.

The origins of ticket collecting on 'Omnibuses' certainly date back to stagecoach days and, until the advent of computer booking, there remained remarkable similarities between methods of booking and the tickets issued for coach travel whether in 1750, 1850 or 1990. Buses required a quicker method and one where the proprietor could check the honesty (or otherwise) of the fare collector. A box with a simple mechanical counter allowed pennies to be paid in, but this was quickly followed (at least as early as 1875) by ticket issuing - tickets being torn in half, pre-numbered, with part being issued as a receipt; the other being handed in by the conductor together with a waybill and the appropriate cash. The use of the bell punch (normal after 1893) which punched a hole in the ticket while giving its characteristic 'ting' reduced fraud; the bell does not sound until a ticket is punched. However, it was a poor or odd conductor who could not cover the driver's and his tea from 'mislaid' fares. During the 1920s it was not unusual for a driver, conductor and a bus to be sent out to find new routes. The first charge on the revenue was their petrol, the second their grub and accommodation, thirdly their wages and only then did the company expect a return.

The Bell Punch Co. advertisement is dated 17th January, 1935 when, alas, the terrible slump in trade and hence poverty-inducing unemployment still had two years to run, but it was a good New Year's wish. Although tickets, racks, and leather accoutrements were purchased by the operator, most, if not all, bell punch type machines were leased at a rate in the 1920s of about £1 10s. per annum each.

The sheer variety of tickets that were in use during the 'Bell Punch' era makes their collection quite exciting geographically and they are still cheap. What other historically valuable item from the 1890s can you get for £5?

Most companies were very proud of their ability to service and repair almost any bus in their fleet. Pre-war a complete overhaul was required after four years' life and the vehicle was considered as written off after seven. This was particularly true of light-engined American machines, while wooden-framed bodies were rattled apart by the (often cobbled) road surface of the 1920s and 1930s. Chassis design evolved and what was shiny new in 1931 was an old nail by 1937. East Kent Central Works, Kirby's Lane, Canterbury, 1938.

The M&D and East Kent Bus Club

Obviously wartime affected bus operation in various ways. Some companies - particularly those on the coast - saw their seasonal traffic disappear while others in the mining and manufacturing areas suffered gross overload. To meet these difficulties some regulations were relaxed but others, the lack of lighting, blacked out windows and unfamiliar interior bus seating layouts affected even 'old hand' conductors, let alone the newcomers drafted in. One result was the use of volunteer auxiliary conductors who, in exchange for free travel on the trip they worked (a 'concession' not a right), saw

to platform duties while the conductor collected the fares. This badge, issued by West Hartlepool Corporation Transport, is a rare survivor and, although issued in the darkest days of war, is enamelled in a glorious iridescent red. A similar scheme in Manchester required the auxiliaries to call out the names of bus stops while Stockton-on-Tees divided up their 60 volunteers into 10 groups who, whenever they had spare time, helped the conductresses, although after 1942 they also had a roster. Leeds and Manchester had a variant on normal duties inasmuch as not only did the volunteers 'guard' the platform but had that most unpleasant of jobs - queue marshalling. *Above:* Driver, clippie, wartime paintwork on the bus. He is wearing his gas mask while she, seemingly, is about to try hers out. There was a real fear of gas attacks, most of the public knew of the results of such ghastliness in World War I.

Different types of emergency canteens were put into use during wartime. These were installed in suitable locations either after existing facilities became overloaded or for various reasons were non-existent. With rationing strictly enforced and given the difficulties the crews had getting home, these canteens allowed operators to still run split shifts and reduce dissatisfaction. Since a split shift could be 6.00-9.00 am, 11.30 am – 2.00 pm, 4.00-8.00 pm (timing that still existed as late as the 1960s), the temptation for the crews to skip the evening rush hour was vast. ADU 407 of the East Kent fleet (ex-Isle of Thanet Electric Supply Company) was a 1934 Daimler COG5 with Weymann 56-seat bodywork acquired in 1937. It was converted to a mobile canteen for use at Dover from July 1943, being returned to normal use in November 1944 and surviving until 1958.

In general, when a pre-war bus was built the anticipated life was seven years. This was understood both by the licensing authorities and the operators; re-licensing was required after seven years and it was rarely worth the anticipated rebuilding. AJG 5 was a Leyland Titan TD5 with Park Royal 53-seater bodywork delivered in 1938 to the East Kent Road Car Company and therefore in the normal course of events would be scrapped in 1945. This view shows the bus surveying bomb damage at Dover in 1943, although from 1940 to 1942 it had been loaned to East Kent's sister company, the Lincolnshire RCC. Withdrawn in 1951, the machinery of AJG 5 was used in a Beadle semi-chassisless coach, not finally scrapped until the late 1960s. In the meantime thrifty East Kent re-used the body on JG 8241, another TD4 of an earlier batch, this then surviving until 1953.
(Both) The M&D and East Kent Bus Club

Wartime photographs other than hackneyed 'officials' are not too common. Bomb damage varied from total to light, this is St Peter's Depot, Broadstairs, after a hit-and-run raid in 1943. The nearest bus, AJG 5 (again), a Leyland TD5 with 1938 Park Royal body, shows the compulsory masked headlights and white rimmed wings.
M&D and East Kent Bus Club

The same bus appears in this photograph, also dated 1943, showing evacuation of schoolchildren from the vehicle to the shelter (note the 'S' indicator) at Canterbury bus station. Although white lining around the bus remains, window anti-blast netting no longer exists.
M&D and East Kent Bus Club

During the war the Government, faced with U-boats sinking tankers faster than they could be built, restricted fuel oil supplies to the bare minimum and required that experiments were to be carried out on alternative fuels. By 1941 they recommended the use of 30 per cent creosote mixed with 80 octane petrol and vastly increased research into producer gas operations. Most companies were half-hearted in their approach but in the main adapted handfuls of petrol-engined vehicles - typically East Kent tried five double-deckers. The gas given off from heating anthracite was rather impure and it was difficult to keep a draught into the burner in town work (the hotter the firebox the better the gas) but vehicles ran out of 'puff' on country hills. These views show an East Kent Leyland TD1 coupled to an oil burner.

(Both) The M&D and East Kent Bus Club

Midland Red (BMMO) variant together with a very valid warning; RAF cyclists hitching a ride found this very valid!

The alternative to producer gas generation, town gas, as seen in use here on a Burnley, Colne and Nelson Leyland was very unpopular due to its smell, propensity to shrapnel damage and adverse effects on vehicle handling in windy conditions.
East Pennine Transport Group

The Bedford OWB (W = Wartime) was a derivative of Bedford's (née Vauxhall Motors) pre-war and post-war 'OB' types. During the hostilities Bedford's produced over 250,000 vehicles (including 5,000 tanks) and in 1941 the OB was chosen as a basis for wartime single-deck PSV production. Long since moved away from its parent General Motors Chevrolet, the OB chassis was simple, strong and powered by a petrol engine of some ruggedness. The outline of the wartime body was rigidly specified and included 32 wooden-slatted seats. These had been replaced and austerity bodywork details softened when this Windsorian OWB was photographed in 1947 on hire to London Transport for trips to Windsor Castle (*seen here*) and the Great Park.

During wartime, all countries are forced to produce for the home market economy vehicles using 'base' metals this saving non-ferrous materials for more essential purposes and these so called utility or ersatz machines were also designed to be labour-saving. There appears to be an accord among photographers that all buses are viewed from the front three-quarter angle only and yet to show the full glory of GLX 905, a Daimler CWA 6 with Duple 1945 bodywork, we need to see the rear roof and 'dome' to understand its utility construction; one requiring no skilled input from panel beaters who would be engaged on aircraft component bashing. Once D19 in the London Transport fleet, GLX 905 passed to Brown's Blues of Markfield, Leicestershire, in 1954, and was scrapped in 1958. The polished radiator surround was a replacement; the mini-headlights original. *Richard Butler*

The Thomas Tilling fleet used in London was built between 1930 and 1932 and incorporated a quite outmoded open staircase. ST 849 (as re-numbered after passing to London Transport) was photographed by Alan Cross on 11th December, 1948, by which time its bodywork was sagging and it had become a driver trainer.

Alan B. Cross

The wartime photograph of an unknown numbered sister vehicle shows not only the exposed staircase, but the wartime anti-blast netting with tiny peepholes and the blue-painted upstairs windows. The white bull's eye was to help motorists running on one dim headlight see this vehicle at night. In this mollycoddled age can you imagine unaccompanied small boys going to school in wartime and peering over this staircase? Great fun; like 'The Gods' at the cinema!

1933 Leyland Tiger TS6 with MCW bodywork at Berwick just post-war. H93J was one of over 50 built to this design; rebodied in 1949 this machine ran until 1960. Notice the SMT logo in the background.

Two Bedfords from Geoff Amos' fleet, typifying the transition from wartime utility bus bodywork (JVX 307) to luxury coachwork (JAF 832) although both had similar Bedford engines and chassis.

Bus Resurgent - The 1940s

A fascinating line-up of Pontypridd UDC vehicles at their depot. Left to right we have an unknown utility bus, then No. 18, a Bristol K5G/BBW built in 1942, No. 33 a Guy Arab II 5LW/Park Royal of 1943, No. 39, another Bristol but type K6A/Park Royal 1944, No. 37, another Arab of the same batch as 33, but delivered in 1944 and No. 28, a 1939 version of 18. The single-decker nearest the workshop is No. 11 (TG 1953) a Bristol B type with unusual Eastwood & Kenning bodywork, new 1931 and scrapped 1949. In the workshop is No. 40, sister to No. 39.   *Omnibus Society*

By way of contrast, an East Kent fleet view taken at Canterbury 1940, when these pre-war Leyland Tiger TS7 with Park Royal coach bodies had been converted to ambulances, initially for use after Dunkirk, but also to cope with bombing casualties. Visible are Nos. 43, 40, 35, 42, 45, all new in 1935 and withdrawn (after reversion to civilian guise) in 1955.

Left: There were a surprising number of differences between a standard Leyland Titan PD2 and the RTW class built for London Transport - even the chassis frame was of AEC profile - but an order for 500 chassis and bodies was not to be foregone, and the company were quite happy to rework both their chassis and body designs to suit. Undoubtedly the major difference between these vehicles and all others within the RT-style fleet was their 8 ft width rather than the normal 7 ft 6 in.; indeed many tests were carried out before permission was given to operate these giants. This extra width was used to make the gangway four inches and the seats one inch wider. This is RTW 1, chassis 6RT 472472 undergoing her tilt test at the Leyland Works, 4th February, 1949.

Below: A beautiful, if poignant, study of an elderly tram doing what they did best and the usurper, an RTL unusually carrying its full blind display. Roger Kidner, in his *The London Tramcar* has written that '. . . at the time of its demise the London tram was already an anachronism: a vehicle which deposited its passengers in the middle of the road, and announced its progress by clanging a bell like a muffin man'. But given the cash and the will, they could have been replaced by modern vehicles running in reserved paths, the RTL and her sisters serving as stop-gaps while the work was carried out - after all, even the best buses are relatively ephemeral entities.   *C. Carter*

Two photographs of similar vehicles, showing both how liveries can vary between two operators and how the camera can, in monochrome, be 'blind' to some colours. Both buses are products of their time, 1945, when austerity ruled every aspect of peoples' lives, to a degree quite unimaginable today. The top one BEA 721, was No. 121 in the fleet of West Bromwich Corporation Transport, whose vehicles were noted for their smartness, especially when it will be recollected that West Bromwich was an area noted for heavy manufacturing industry with its concomitant grime. No. 121 was a Daimler CWA 6 with Brush 56-seat 'relaxed utility' bodywork - not quite so basic as earlier but still severe in outline and trim. Mildly rebuilt by the Corporation this bus was quite magnificent in its two-tone (light/dark) blue and cream paintwork enhanced by fine gold lining out, a credit to A. Witcomb Smith, the General Manager.

No. 130, VV 8992 of the Northampton Transport fleet is also a Daimler, albeit a Daimler-engined CWD 6 with Duple bodywork, differing by only a few details, and similarly rebuilt in 1952 and, curiously, being finally withdrawn the same year, 1960, as No. 121. However this bus and the Roe-bodied Daimler behind it is in the warm red and cream livery adopted by Northampton, but reds are notoriously unstable and this has dulled. Remember conductresses? This one, on the right, is clutching her waybill and Ultimate ticket machine, her cash bag resting on her right hip, as she looks for her relief.

Municipalities employed some of the best bus engineers in the United Kingdom, if not the world, and given the need for constraint in expenditure and the variable quality of their drivers it is no wonder they chose good, reliable, traditional (in the best sense of the word) vehicles. Walsall No. 115 was a 1949-delivered Guy Arab III with Gardner 5-cylinder engine and Park Royal bodywork, the only eccentricities being the shape of the blind apertures and the improbable powder blue paintwork. Behind is one of their bargains, an ex-London Transport Leyland 7RT with Park Royal LT-style bodywork built 1954 and barely run in when purchased by Walsall in 1959. No. 203 (Ex-RTL 1487, OLD 596) survived until 1971.

Richard Butler

In 1933 a new General Manager, R.A. Fearnley, was appointed to the Coventry Corporation Transport fleet and like all new brooms brought a new look. Very quickly (and logically, as they were made in Coventry) he adopted Daimler chassis, but as he was an AEC man by inclination he had these fitted with AEC diesel engines, whilst retaining the Daimler pre-selective gearboxes. Trams were steadily eliminated but as a standard bus rarely seated more than 54 he developed in conjunction with MCW a super-lightweight body seating 60 - although in some discomfort. No. 70 was delivered in 1949 and withdrawn in 1967. Behind is another Daimler, although Gardner-engined, still a Fearnley-inspired machine but now (1959) with MCW 'Orion' bodywork, still seating 60 but of a style famously described as a 'monstrous mass of shivering tin'!

GOE 648 was a bus of typically Birmingham outline and it was a fact of bus life (and part of the charm) that when a large fleet like the BCT cracked their fingers, chassis and bodybuilders alike jumped to produce whatever was required. This is a Crossley of Erwood, Lancs., product delivered 1949 and withdrawn in 1964. The great advantage of a back loader was never more clearly demonstrated. Behind is 5045 HA, an equally typical 'Midland Red' (Birmingham & Midland Motor Omnibus Co.) outline with recessed driver's windscreen, clear blinds and utilitarian plainness around the front. This bus was assembled in 1962 on a home-built S15 chassis utilizing Carlyle bodywork. Carlyle works were the bodybuilding arm of the BMMO and they fitted this batch 5045-5092 with dual purpose (bus/coach) seating. Quite short-lived, No. 5045 was withdrawn in 1973 but is seen here running towards Digbeth after completion of an express run from Ashby-de-la-Zouch.

When vehicles get superseded they can gain a new lease of life in the service fleet. This battered relic, a 1928 Brush-bodied Southdown Leyland, performed the essential duty of tree-lopper; an aspect of bus operation often overlooked today when boughs can bang the roof and windows to the dismay of passengers.

W.J. Haynes

The blind of an immaculate FAY 517 in the fleet of Brown's Blue Coaches Ltd shows Stanton under Bardono, a village nine miles north-west of Leicester but one would need local knowledge for any intermediate points on the journey. Bodywork was by Brush of Loughborough on a Daimler chassis of the type CVD 6. The 'V' stood for Victory even though the bus was built in 1949. The garage at Markfield is typical of a medium sized operator.

Brown's Blue Coaches Ltd of Markfield, Leicestershire, commenced operations in 1923, became the largest operator in the county by 1963 with 70 employees and 39 vehicles, but in that year they sold out to Midland Red. Sixteen stage carriage ('bus') routes were operated and a heterogeneous mixture of vehicles could appear on them. Just off route 15 (Leicester-Whitwick) is EAY 180, a Leyland PS1/1 with Yeates coach body new in 1947, HAY 111 on route 16 (Measham) is an AEC Regal IV with Gurney Nutting body, and GUT 400 (one of three alike) on Route 7 is another Regal IV but with Yeates bodywork. None of these concerns are involved in vehicle manufacture today although Yeates is a very successful dealer. Photographed 1959.

THE BRISTOL TRAMWAYS & CARRIAGE COMPANY, LIMITED.

No. 274

1/3, ST. AUGUSTINE'S PLACE,
BRISTOL, 30th. DECEMBER, 1944.

TO

SIR J.FREDERICK HEATON,
BOVINGDON GRANGE,
BOVINGDON,HERTS.

6

A cheque in payment of the amount due to you as under has, in accordance with
your instructions, been sent to your bankers.

	Shares	£	s	d
Dividend for the half-year ended **31st. December, 1944** on 4% Preference Shares	500	10	0	0
Less Income Tax @ 10/- in the £		5	0	0
£		5	0	0

I hereby certify that the amount of Income Tax as set forth in this statement has been, or will be, paid by
the Company to the proper Officer for the receipt of taxes. This statement will be accepted by the Inland
Revenue as proof of payment of the tax in claiming exemption from or return of Income Tax.

R. E. ARMSTRONG, *Secretary.*

It was, perhaps, a sign of their confidence that senior officers in the great pre-war companies purchased additional shares in their own concerns instead of sitting back and just taking their 'freebies'. John Frederick Heaton was the Chairman of a group of British Electric Traction (BET) companies including the Bristol Tramways & Carriage Company from 1935. Knighted in 1942 he was to remain in control until 1948. Major Francis J. Chapple was the General Manager of Bristol Tramways and a Director of BET and had a reputation as a hard but fair man. The income tax rate of 50 per cent was one that applied during the war, being reduced to a mere 45 per cent for the year 1946-47.

1	Jan|Feb|Mar|Apr|May|June|July|Aug|Sep|Oct|Nov|Dec
2	THE WESTERN NATIONAL OMNIBUS CO., LTD.
3	THE SOUTHERN NATIONAL OMNIBUS CO.,LTD.
4	**DUTY ONLY PRIVILEGE PASS** (Available only on Stage Carriage Services and only to and from place of residence and employment.)
5	Issued to .... Staff
6	BLOCK CAPITALS No. ....
7	Depot .... Dept. ....
8	No. X
	This Pass must be shown on every journey.
9	DATE OF EXPIRY .... 194...
10	Available between .... and .... only.
11	Signature of holder ....
	This Pass is the property of the Company and must be surrendered upon leaving the Company's service for any cause or on demand by the Company.
12	**NOT TRANSFERABLE.**
13	Date of Issue .... 194...
14	Issued by .... Head Office : QUEEN STREET, EXETER

The Northern General
Transport Co., Ltd.

**EMPLOYEES' WIFE'S HALF
FARE SERVICE PASS.**

NOT TRANSFERABLE.

No. 1356

Name ....

Husband's Grade ....

Date of issue ....

For the Northern General Transport
Co., Ltd.

....

General Manager.

CONDITIONS.

1. This pass is issued to an employee for use by an employee's wife only, and entitles the holder or any children accompanying holder to travel on Northern service omnibuses and routes north of Durham and south of Newcastle at half the ordinary return fare, excepting where odd halfpennies occur, when the additional halfpenny will be charged in each case. Minimum fare under this concession 4d.

2. That it be produced whenever demanded by the Conductor or any duly authorised Officer of the Company.

3. That the Company shall not be held liable for any damage or injury sustained by the holder when travelling on any service omnibuses.

4. That on the employee terminating his service with the Company, this Pass be returned to the Office from which it was issued.

Working for a large concern gave uniforme staff the advantage of quite reasonable trav facilities, especially where the company ha wide ranging destinations. Typically, a ma might have four passes each year for himsel and family to travel either free or at 25 pe cent of the full rate. On a tour it might well b that the coach element was free and only th accommodation paid for with a 10 per cer discount on this. Conversely as an employe of a small company it was normal for one family to travel free as and when require although perhaps the furthest 'run' was to th market town. Some concerns, particularly i later years, have had reciprocal arrangemen with other companies, thus again widenin the scope for travel.

AW Nọ̈   5265

D. G. O. & T. Co., Ltd.

9d.   Receipt
Parcel

Parcels only accepted subject to the regulations and conditions shown on notices displayed at Company's Offices and Agents.

United Counties Omnibus Co. Ltd.
BUS PARCELS SERVICE
Prepaid Parcel
Receipt   9d

At Owner's Risk and subject to Company's Regulations contained in Official Time-Tables and Notices.

A75797

B 7339

WILTS. & DORSET
Motor Services Ltd.

PARCEL
2d

DEMURRAGE

For rates and conditions of carriage see Company's official time table books.

Williamson, Printer, Ashton
W49

CROSVILLE MOTOR SERVICES LTD.
Bulk Prepaid Newspaper Stamp

Up to Seven Miles **2d**	ISSUED SUBJECT TO PARCEL REGULATIONS AS SET OUT IN THE COMPANY'S OFFICIAL GUIDE

H 0184

Williamson, Ticket Printer, Ashton-u-Lyne

BARTON
TRANSPORT LTD.
PARCEL TICKET
6d
Nọ̈ 851 1 C
PAID

Parcels are carried subject to Company's Regulations relating to conveyance of parcels

E55404

UNITED COUNTIES
ONMIBUS CO. LTD.

BUS
PARCELS   9d
SERVICE

All parcels carried at Owner's Risk and subject to Co's regulations contained in Official Time Tables and Notices.

Williamson, Ticket Printer, Ashton

Letter transport was strictly prohibited, but not unknown, whereas parcel working before the days of common car ownership could embarrass some operators especially when running buses full and standing. Still, everyone mucked in somehow although in 1942 Scottish Motor Traction asked to be allowed to stop carrying fruit 'under the parcels transmission scheme, which is a feature of its bus services'. Payment methods varied between the bright red three-part stickers of Edinburgh, to a more homely treatment where the 'tanner' (6d.) was shared between driver and conductor as a 'perk', such arrangements being winked at by the employer to compensate for low wages. Obviously the larger the company the more parcels carrying was regulated with special rates applying for regular traffics. Some of the variety in the tickets issued is shown; but the days of a handful of sweeties given to the conductor to drop something off for Mrs Davies at the Post Office are long gone, alas.

Luck can play a part in deciding whether a vehicle goes off to the great scrapyard in the sky or if it is to have a second life. HYP 697 had an unusual Commer Commando chassis with Park Royal bodywork which despite appearances could only carry 18 passengers; the rest of the space being required to hold the baggage of trans-continental passengers. Australia was in 1947, when 364F was built, a matter of days away - even in 1959 it was still a 37 hour journey! Withdrawn in 1952 HYP remained in airline service but with Skyways at Stansted airport. In 1995 we were told that one of this class of coach was in use with 'travellers' in a rather remote part of Shropshire. The owner was very proud of his conversion and that he was preserving this piece of airline history. By April 1996 they were gone - perhaps it rolls along yet . . .

The Golden Age of the '50s

The Birch family entered the road transport business in London as cab operators in 1832. Their first motor bus arrived as early as 1904, but in 1934 the London Passenger Transport Board compulsorily purchased all their routes in London so that they were forced to expand their services in the Bedford direction. Their main route, the 203, is depicted here in 1949. Although the blinds of this home-built body (on a Leyland PD1 chassis) are large, the cant of the body front (directly opposite to that of the Nottingham vehicle) made them difficult to read from the bus stop. Birch Bros were to sell out to the Ewer Group in 1971.

Read here a fable. Once upon a time there was a Corporation transport fleet, smart and loved by all who came into contact with it, with neat buses crewed by the most pleasant and courteous crews one could meet. HEY 722 was a Leyland PD2/12 built in 1952 with an elegant well fitted Weymann body, even the mudguards were the right height for leaning on! The end of the fable? Oh, Southport the town and its buses alike were swallowed by the Merseyside dragon.

The Recruit

EVERY NEW BUS *for London Transport has to pass many tests and inspections before it can qualify for a road licence.*

The new bus, after the completion of the maker's tests, is driven to our Aldenham Works, where London Transport engineers give it a critical examination. After this it is paraded for the Ministry of Transport Certifying Officer. Each bus is inspected and strictly measured. The readings are checked against the official figures—its length, width, both inside and out, the distance between the seats, its height from the road and so on. When these measurements are agreed the whole bus is weighed—it must not weigh more than 12 tons fully loaded—and it is then given a final road test before being delivered to one of the 110 London Transport garages and depots.

But whenever a new type of bus is introduced, one from the first batch undergoes a still more rigorous examination and is tested under conditions far more severe than it will ever meet when carrying passengers.

Both the Ministry of Transport and London Transport must be sure that the recruit is sound in wind and limb before he goes into service. And it is not until they are completely satisfied that the bus is given its road licence and can begin its working life.

The numerically largest fleet of similar buses to enter service in Britain was the Regent Type (RT) class of London Transport. The chassis of the prototype, a joint venture between LT and AEC, was delivered to the Chiswick Works of London Transport on 23rd May, 1938. After experiments and modifications it was fitted with the prototype body which in essence provided the outline for the class. The first production batch, RT2-151, had composite bodies with hardwood pillars and were completed by May 1940, although the chassis were held back as materials for war took precedence, RT151 entering service in January 1942. Two external distinctions marked out these pre-war ordered vehicles, the drooping windscreen and cab side window - aids to visibility but expensive - and the provision of roof top destination boxes fore and aft. RT11 and RT12 are facing us, the rear is probably that of RT141.

The London Transport engineers were rightly proud of this family of vehicles, which at their peak, 1954, included 146 pre-war survivors, 4,674 post-war AEC deliveries, 1,630 modified Leyland PD9 of the RTL class, and 500 8 ft wide all-Leyland RTWs. But not even LT engineers could have dreamed that 50 years after they were built numbers would still appear on rally fields, in some cases after having second or third owners. On 'Railway Emergency Service' is RT3241 showing four of her blinds.

In the fleet of Brown's Blues is ex-RT179.

The Samuel Ledgard MXX 149 is ex-RT3634.

The preserved machine is RT1431 on the annual Southport to Blackpool run. FDT 43C is a 1965 ex-Doncaster Roe-bodied Leyland RTC1/1 also preserved.

Our main purpose in life is to carry passengers. If we are to keep going in the highly competitive world in which we now live we must do all in our power to maintain and improve the standard of service we offer to Londoners. I know that we can rely on you and the staff under you to maintain London Transport's reputation as the finest undertaking of its kind in the world. We are part of London and proud of it.

(From the Chairman Sir John Elliot's 1956 message to senior staff)

To many people photographs like this show vehicles that epitomised the great days of London Transport, 55 Broadway. Sir John Elliot's last sentence was quite right, of course.

As is right and proper on the 7th February, 1959 RT4359 waits for 395, a D2 class trolleybus, running off route 698 to turn into Bexleyheath Depot. Some may say that the overhead wires are intrusive but given that any trolleybus was almost noiseless save for a thrum of tyres and the clicking of the contactor gear, how much better than a diesel's snarl and fumes. But who are we transport people to stand in the way of financiers' progress?   *A.D. Packer*

Rush-hour. There is harmony between the outline of the RT, the bus stop, the public and the buildings in the far background. The bus design that would harmonize with the block on the left doesn't bear thinking about. Gloomily one must add that the front dome of the bus bears witness to the decline in London Transport standards.

One of the greatest examples of London Transport's resilience occurred in 1951, when they provided the special services required for the Festival of Britain. Five years after the end of World War II the LTE had hardly begun to get to grips with the lack of wartime maintenance and although many post-war buses had been delivered these totalled only 50 per cent of those required for their normal services. Opened 4th May, 1951, on the South Bank of the Thames on what had been a 27 acre scene of desolation and bomb damage, eight special routes were involved to give good access to the Exhibition buildings from the Underground and railway stations. In all (including private hire work and supplementary 'ordinary' services) 137 buses were found in use at any time until the cessation of the exhibition after 20th September. This is STL1621 on the first day waiting at York Road, Waterloo. — *J.H. Meredith*

Atmospheric days in Birmingham. In common with most cities in the 1950s Birmingham suffered from chemical fog as the smoke from coal-burning fireplaces and coal-fired boilers collided with a damp day. Seen through the murk of Navigation Street is a Leyland PD2/1 fleet No. 2159 (JOJ 159), its Leyland-built body providing (by today's standards) precious little comfort or warmth. Delivered March 1949, 2159 was not withdrawn until 1967, by which time the smogs of a decade before were only a memory.

PHONE 250

Giant, Car and
Tractor Tyres
always in Stock

THOMAS JOHNSTON & SON

AUTOMOBILE ENGINEERS

Registered Service
Dealers for Giant
and Car Tyres

JOHNSTON'S TYRE DEPOT

DALBEATTIE

JMcL/IH   15th December, 1950.

Mr. G. K. Wrigley,
48 Haslingden Drive,
HEATON,
Bradford,
Yorks.

Dear Sir,

     Prior to the 1939-45 war, we did run Service between
Colvend and Castle Douglas, but this Service was terminated
by us due to economic conditions. We have pleasure how:
:ever, in detailing below Time Tables of the existing Ser:
:vices which we hope you will find suitable.

     We assure you of our best attention at all times.

                  Yours faithfully,
          pro: THOMAS JOHNSTON AND SON.

Weekdays Only (Winter)

Penmans Service - (Sandyhills, Colvend & Dalbeattie)

Leave Sandyhills	- 9.30am	12.30pm	4.30pm
Arrive Dalbeattie	-10 AM	1.00pm	5.00pm
Leave Dalbeattie	- 8.45am	11.45am	3.45pm
Arrive Sandyhills	- 9.15am	12.15am	4.15pm

Western S.M.T. Service (Kippford, Dalbeattie & Castle Douglas

Leave Kippford	9.45am	11.55am	5.50pm
Arrive Dalbeattie	10am	12.10pm	6.05pm
Leave Dalbeattie	10am	12.15pm	6.20pm
Arrive Castle-Douglas	10.25am	12.40pm	6.45pm
Leave Castle-Douglas	11.10am	5.10pm	
Arrive Dalbeattie	11.35am	5.35pm	
Arrive Kippford	11.55am	5.50pm	

For how long, and how well, a route ran is affected by all manner of outside influences - in my time the loss of cinema traffic and later school swimming bath visits, both of which required vehicles to be used (and hence earn money) in otherwise idle periods, has caused as many companies to cease trading as has the loss of contract work to motor-car companies, mines or steelworks, themselves disastrous cutbacks for many bus firms. Silver Service of Darley Dale ran to an almost unchanged timetable from 1932 to 1972 but within a year the Trent Motor Traction company had completely replaced Silver Service in their heartland services to Rowsley and Youlgreave, simply because Trent had taken over the local North Western operations. The North Western shared work with Silver Service, while Trent competed. The letter explains all too clearly the problems of a country concern.

AA Motor Services of Ayr had a complex birth but was a 1930 grouping or co-operative of independents operating on the Ayr-Ardrossan route. This vehicle is DT No. 5 owned (within the group) by W. Dodds (Dodds Coaches Ltd) of Troon. DGG 910 has a 1943 Guy Arab II chassis, rebodied by Roe in 1953 with an unusual centre entrance bus body fitted with dual-purpose seats.

At the time of this photograph Stanhope Motor Services 'main line' was from Stanhope to Wearhead, although being associated with Weardale Motor Services of Frosterley they interworked with their routes. The whole Weardale Valley is probably one of the most inhospitable for bus operation, running as it does between (1,300-1,600 ft) hills on either side.

R.B. Parr

The Dunbar Veteran & Vintage Rally has always been well attended by 'foreign' vehicles, not the least those coming from Northern Ireland. Here D927, a 1950 Leyland PD2/1 with Ulster Transport Authority bodywork, is seen driving off the Sealink Larne/Stranraer ferry *Dalriada* in 1975.

British Rail

Burnley Colne & Nelson No. 37 was a standard 1953 Leyland PS2 with an East Lancs body. As conductors became too expensive to carry so this body was converted to one-person-operation in 1959 - the angled window is clearly visible.

Coventry bus station, now demolished.

Although the London Transport driving school, including as it did the use of a skidpan, was incomparable there is no doubt that all Corporation training was thorough. They had the advantage that elderly vehicles were available (some still in fleet use) and thus would-be drivers could learn the charms of uninsulated cabs, muleish steering, all too often bad visibility, 'iffy' brakes (if you're lucky they do, if not . . .) and the weird habits of the public. Coventry Corporation had seven vehicles on offer here, as all too many men either left to go coaching or just left when the wife complained about the unsocial hours. 06 (GKV 55), 09 (GKV 69) and 00 (FHP 19) are those visible; all Daimlers with AEC engines built 1948 (00) and 1949 (06, 09).

By contrast Burnley & Pendle had only one single-decker, an East Lancs-bodied Leyland Tiger Cub built in 1959 and used as a semi-preserved trainer from 1986.

Cumberland with its ECW-bodied Bristol assumed that passers-by knew a bus was a PSV.   *C.W. Routh*

At one time United Automobile Services Ltd, had most of North East England for itself, although in unpopulated areas (the National Park measures 400 square miles and in 1992 had 23,000 cattle, 303,000 sheep and 2,000 people) independents were left to scratch a living. Moffit of Hexham was one of these. The 'clippie' is one of the family and dustcoats were regulation wear.

The interiors of buses should really have received more attention than they got until relatively recently. It is true that unlike a coach the faster the turnover of 'bums on seats' the better for revenue but mostly seating has been the province more of the engineer than designer. Even back in the 1920s the problem was always to find the balance between 'crowding 'em [the passengers] in when they're going to work and gettin' them in with their shopping'. Always there were passengers who got market 'peart' and lost their lunch and

vandals who loved slashing seats. Many were the bedraggled city buses that emerged in the morning with the upper deck rear seats in ribbons and floors reeking of Lysol or Jeyes fluid, so strong it could even make dockers weep and hurriedly light their shag-filled pipes. Wooden seats for miners were still about in the 1950s and the yellow nicotine-impregnated condensation dripping from the ceilings was proof of missing heating. This selection shows nice new shiny interiors. The information was always displayed; seating and standing capacities were governed by the inability of conductors to collect fares, national and local byelaws and by the weight limits imposed by the chassis manufacturers.

This 1923 East Kent Tilling-bodied Tilling-Stevens TS6 has wooden-framed seats, lightweight framing, but leather-covered squabs, quite good lighting for the period, but few if any bell-pushes. The roof is omitted to aid the photographer.   *The M&D and East Kent Bus Club*

The Brush body of North Western Road Car No. 1520 dates back to the 1930s and is for one-man-operation on a Leyland chassis; 20 moquette-covered wooden-framed seats and a painted ceiling. Unusually good ventilation, although this pincer type of window catch was prone to jamming and cock-billing, leaving a howling draught from the front to the back of the bus. The remote door operation is by way of the rod running from door to dash and a lever; instruments include speedo, oil temperature and pressure gauges, together with an ammeter.

An official photograph of an experimental Bristol Lodekka (XC 102/1) was taken in December 1957 at the grandiloquently named Motor Construction Works, Brislington, to show the new cowls in the lower saloon. The intention was to reduce these as far as possible as they made sitting on the lengthwise benches a somewhat inelegant arrangement for be-frocked girls. Although serviceable enough the layout is remarkably fussy and was improved in production vehicles.

Wallasey Corporation fleet No. 69 delivered November 1951, a Leyland Titan PD2/12 with Metro-Cammell-Weymann bodywork, of a style typical of the time. Leather upholstery, lino insert panel in the bulkhead, but slatted (and unbelievably difficult to clean) floor, tungsten bulbs and handgrips for straphangers. This particular batch were the first 8 ft wide vehicles delivered to Wallasey and the first to have a pale green decor.

The Leyland-MCW integral Olympic first introduced in 1949 is represented by this HR 40 (Home Range, 40 seat) short length model (27 ft 6 in.) delivered in 1950 to Red & White of Chepstow. The engine was a Leyland 0.600 of 9.8 litres capacity developing a nominal 130 bhp and among other claims was that 'if necessary, the complete unit can be removed, replaced and started up in less than one hour'. But withstanding this and the inherent strength of the MCW body the traditional body/chassis construction proved to be more popular, the Olympic ceasing to be available in 1957. Luggage racks require the 'mind your heads' labels on seat backs and almost inevitably spitting is 'strictly prohibited'. The heater on the bulkhead and air pressure ceiling ventilation were plus factors on a cold Welsh winter night!   *Chris Taylor*

Badges of authority or commendation were always a part of a bus crew's life, and were as varied as the companies who employed them. All reputable companies issued some form of 'Rule Book' and this was no bad thing insofar as working within this kept many bus crews out of trouble. My London Transport Rulebook was issued in 1953 and states 'Employees must wear their uniform, cap and licence badges, and equipment at all times when on duty' while Leicester by 1981 stated 'drivers are permitted to wear their own anorak type jackets . . . and in summer you may dispense with a jacket provided you are wearing a plain shirt without gaudy patterns'. Back in 1953 'Drivers and conductors must wear their white cap covers from 1st May to 30th September inclusive'.

Cap badge: SMT Conductor. Nickel-plated brass.
Cap badge: 15 years service, Western National. Red, cream and white enamel with gold lettering.
Cap badge: Devon General, Gold on red lustre enamel.

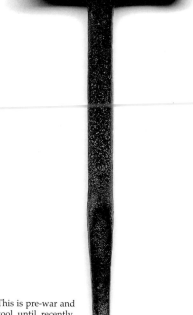

Right: Budget or T-key. This is pre-war and an absolutely essential tool until recently. Used to unlock almost anything (blinds, first aid box, boot, light fittings, etc.) on a bus.

A splendid portrait of PDW 250, a Bedford SB with Duple body operated by Jenkins of Newport.

An official photograph of Seagull coaches' Burlingham 'Seagull'. Probably the only time when a coach-body was given a type-name based on that of the operator.

Two Fordson 7V chassis were bodied by Bellhouse Hartwell. The manufacturer's plate dated 26th October, 1950 came from one of these rarities. One of the pair was broken up in the 1970s but the survivor was destroyed to make part of an episode in the ITV Sunday evening soap opera *Heartbeat*.

A ride upon an open-topped bus once set the seal on the quintessential English holiday. The wind might howl across blowing both girls' hair and their skirts awry, halfway round the Grand Tour the promised shower might come and there would be an undignified scramble to get below, but the dear old white bus, sand, salt and spades all made for happy days. East Kent BJG 461, seen here *en route* to Broadstairs. Built to utility standards in 1945 this Park Royal-bodied Guy Arab was cut down in May 1959, and was preserved after withdrawal in 1968.

For an ordinary Birmingham Corporation Transport bus FOP 452 was to lead quite a lively life. Built at the very end of the war with a modified 'Utility' body from a firm who specialized pre-war in coach building, Duple, on a Daimler CWA 6 chassis (itself an oddity as A indicated an AEC rather than Daimler engine). FOP 452 was not to stay in the fleet long, being withdrawn from front line work in 1950 when just five years old. The following year ex-1452 appeared in the Benfleet & District Motor Services fleet, moving then (with B&D's services) to Westcliff-on-Sea MS. In 1955 Southend-on-Sea Corporation Transport acquired a batch of seven Daimlers from Eastern National (all ex-Westcliff-on-Sea Motor Services) including FOP 452 which was then rebuilt and converted to open-top as seen here, re-entering service 1956 on services 67/68 which Southend operated jointly with Eastern National.

Current during 1948/49, this delightful painting proudly bore the title 'Coachwork by Duple'. The location is Jersey airport.

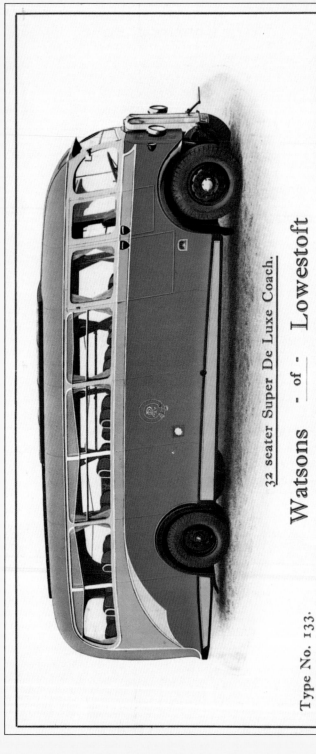

32 seater Super De Luxe Coach.

Watsons - of - Lowestoft

Type No. 133.

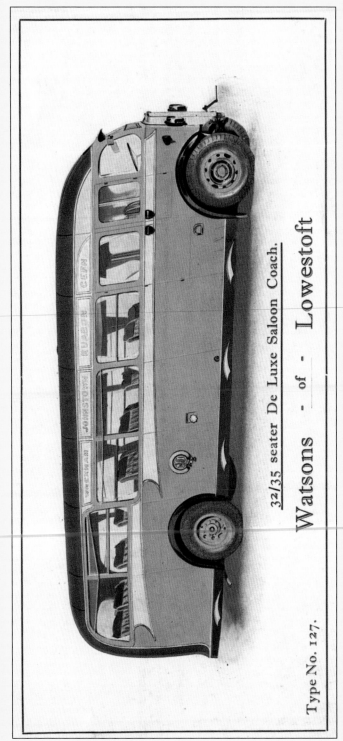

Type No. 127.

Watsons - of - Lowestoft

32/35 seater De Luxe Saloon Coach.

The firm of P.W. Watson & Sons Ltd was founded in Lowestoft during the 1830s and was best known from 1902 onwards for its bodywork on Armstrong-Siddeley, Daimler and Minerva chassises. The firm also owned a fleet of fishing boats! The interior woodwork in its car bodies and coaches was said in the trade to be incomparable. The company was still advertising its skills in 1974.

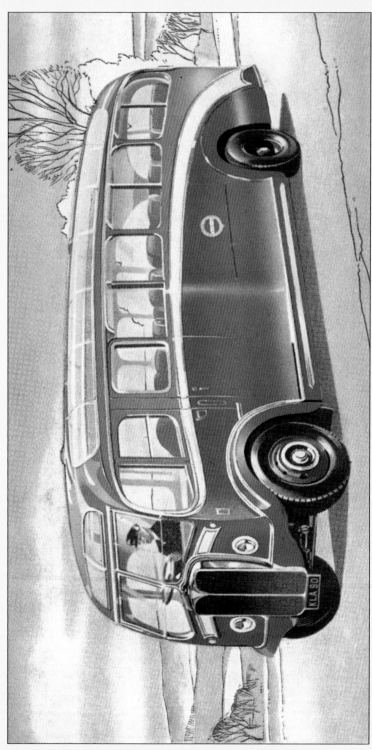

The registration plate on this vehicle was clearly imaginary, 'D' being a 1966 vehicle. Many pre-war chassises were rebodied in the 1940s giving a modern full front while still leaving the exposed (AEC in this case) radiator. Strachans bodywork is fitted.

By 1958 Newcastle-upon-Tyne Corporation had a fleet of 444 public service vehicles, of which 192 were trolleybuses. BUT chassis type 9641 fleet No. 582, a 70-seater, was bodied by Metro-Cammell-Weymann and wears the most improbable of paint colours to find in a city landscape.

Lydney Coachworks commenced operations (as Mumford Body & Engineering Co.Ltd) in 1946 in part of a small wartime-built industrial estate. For various reasons most of the early work offered was cancelled by would-be customers and late deliveries were the norm ensuring few repeat orders being received. Their reputation was hardly enhanced when a batch of 1947 vehicles failed their tilt test, in their as-built condition they were grossly top-heavy. This batch of 12 lowbridge bodies on Leyland PD2/1 chassis were completed during 1949; Lydney Coachworks ceased trading in March 1952.

This rather unusual vehicle of St Helens Corporation Transport carries a Roe dual-purpose (bus/coach) 42-seat body on a powerful AEC Regal IV chassis, and was delivered in February 1951, being withdrawn in 1965, and sold on to Grayshott coaches. The Regal IV chassis was chosen as this vehicle was for use on the long Warrington-Southport service, but in the upshot a restrictive bridge was removed and double-deckers could be utilized instead; 209 remaining unique.

The story of East Midland Motor Services Ltd is incredibly complex - typically from 1929-30 two railways, the LNER and LMSR, jointly owned the company, then selling 51 per cent to the British Electric Traction Company. It is interesting to compare this all-Leyland product with the RTL class of London Transport. Difficult to believe they were products of the same age.

This advertisement is for a Strachans Successors Ltd 'Strathtay' type body, the accompanying write-up commencing: 'Strachans leadership in Coachbuilding is the result of long experience, constant application, attention to detail and the development of true craftsmanship. This craftsmanship will continue to serve Britain's transport of the future with the recognized quality, comfort, convenience and dignity of line built into all Strachans coachwork'.

At one time it was in vogue to have your latest product or acquisition photographed against a 'soft' backdrop. Bedford chassis, costing with oil engine £1,230, Duple Super Vega body, seen at Frensham Ponds, two lakes forming a beauty spot 3½ miles south of Farnham, Surrey.

Between 1949 and 1951 there was a proposal to merge 214 operators, including Stockton, with an overall total of some 4,400 vehicles into one giant concern. Politically motivated, it was dropped when Labour lost their majority in Parliament. Tidy Weymann bodywork is fitted, enhanced by Kearsley's 'Nulac' paintwork.

It is difficult now to remember that in 1955 the East Kent Road Car Company ranked No. 23 in a list of major bus operators in the United Kingdom with 634 vehicles, 280 double-deckers and 354 single-decked buses and coaches. WFN 503 entered service in April 1961 with a Park Royal dual-purpose body having 41 coach seats in a bus (folding door) shell, although the chassis, an AEC Reliance 470, was fast and gave a comfortable ride.

The lower illustration shows GFN 936, having, again, a Park Royal body with 56 seats (30 upstairs with permitted smoking, 26 below) on a Guy Arab IV chassis which ensemble entered service in July 1953. The 'new look' front end with concealed radiator first appeared on Birmingham City Transport's No. 2426 in February 1950, then being quite rapidly specified by many purchasers.

Ribble Motor Services Ltd, whose fleet later incorporated Standerwick and Scout, were one of the most adventurous of the post-war operators, buying a number of less orthodox vehicles. Two batches of double-deck coaches were placed in service during 1949-50, all known as 'White Ladies'. The first 30 (fleet Nos. 1201-1230) were Burlingham products 'leaving little to be desired, for elegance and modernity', even twin 'Perspex' (a clear plastic) sliding sunshine roofs being fitted. On Leyland PD1/3 chassis their Achilles heel seems to have lain in the air-conditioning (ahead of its time) and a relatively old-fashioned chassis. The second tranche were bodied by East Lancashire Coach Builders on PD2/3 chasis; all being later converted to 53-seat stage carriage buses, the last being withdrawn in 1961.

$\mathcal{H}.\mathcal{V}.Burlingham\,Ltd$

BLACKPOOL.

STYLE · QUALITY · CRAFTSMANSHIP

From every angle Strachans coachbuilding expresses leadership—in functional design and a mature understanding of modern styling. This perfect combination springs from long technical experience, superb craftsmanship and an intimate knowledge of the conditions under which modern passenger road transport services operate.
For the best in coachbuilding it pays to specify Strachans.

This marvellous example of un-English exuberance was built by Strachans in 1950 for Highland Transport and exhibited at the Commercial Motor Show. The chassis is a Guy Arab III with lowbridge 57-seat body and was fitted with platform doors for the benefit of passengers (and one might add from bitter experience the conductor too!) and the polished aluminimum trim exuded confidence. An extremely successful all-metal body, Highland might well have bought others had not the company been extinguished by the state-owned Highland Omnibuses. Withdrawn in 1970, 72 passed on to further service elsewhere in Scotland

Although still the classic combination of Bedford SB chassis and Duple bodywork by 1961 the 'Super Vega' had lost the grace and charm of earlier models. A couple of years previously this combination cost, including diesel engine, £3,610 but the same chassis with Burlingham 'Seagull' bodywork was only £70 dearer.

This illustration shows the prototype Guy Wulfrunian chassis with Charles H. Roe of Leeds 75-seat bodywork shortly after delivery in 1959 as No. 863 in the West Riding Automobile Company's fleet. Designed and built by Guy Motors in conjunction with West Riding, a colour oddity was that vehicles used on the old Wakefield tram routes were normally painted red, other vehicles being Mid County Green and Light County Cream. The Wulfrunian was far too advanced with airover-hydraulic disc brakes and independent front air suspension and desperately uncomfortable and hot to drive with a massive Gardner 6LX engine being canted over into the driver's cab. Due to a nose-heavy inbalance four (or more) upper deck front passenger seats were normally removed. In all 156 were built but neither West Riding or Guy Motors had the money to eradicate all its troubles. However two are preserved.

DUPLE CONTINENTAL

36′ 0″ long × 8′ 2⅜″ wide super luxury coach for 51 passengers

TRAVEL IN THE GRAND MANNER

This colour section is not intended to have the effect of photographic work - in the early days of Dufay or early Kodak film with a top speed of 9 DIN or 40 ASA not too many colour photographs of buses and coaches existed, or, at least, were capable of being enlarged and printed. Instead artists' impressions, often hand coloured, sufficed for

Said by many to have been the most attractive coach bodywork ever built, the Harrington Cavalier, depicted here in the late 1950s on an AEC chassis, was to set a standard that lasted for over a decade. The deep curved windscreen greatly enhanced the passengers' view forward, while the fitting of excellent, almost draught-free ventilation, increased comfort, and although having a bright and modern interior the whole package was still incredibly relaxing.

<u>Plaxton</u>

The Plaxton Panorama body was another of the great ground-breaking designs although it took from 1958, when a batch of 'long-bayed' bodies were built for Sheffield United Tours, until the mid-1960s when the fifth version (albeit named Panorama I) appeared as depicted here. Earlier coach designs had been far more curvaceous with six or more ribs dividing up the viewing area, now only three intruded in a relatively square body. Forced ventilation and twin roof hatches replaced draughty drop windows, although later 53-seat versions (rather than the 44-seater shown here) could become incredibly airless in heavy or stationary traffic. Advertisements, too, have finally evolved from the paintings of page 113 to acceptance of photography.

The Swinging Sixties

The blonde clippie appears to be regarding the photographer with some displeasure, perhaps knowing she cannot hope to shine beside this East Lancs body on a Leyland chassis, new in 1962 to the Burnley, Colne & Nelson Joint Transport Committee's fleet.

Take note! An unusual example of notice consolidation is shown on this panel from a Potteries Motor Traction vehicle. Normally individual 'regulations' are to be found scattered all over the front bulkhead(s) and stairwells in a wondrous mixture of printers' type styles and sizes.

THE CONDITIONS UNDER WHICH PASSENGERS ARE CARRIED ARE IN ACCORDANCE WITH THE ROAD TRAFFIC ACT AND PUBLIC SERVICE VEHICLE REGULATIONS.

PASSENGERS ARE REQUESTED TO STATE THEIR DESTINATION AND ARE REQUIRED BY LAW TO PAY THE APPROPRIATE FARE.

STANDING PASSENGERS ARE PERMITTED.

CHILDREN TRAVELLING AT 2/3 FARE SHOULD NOT OCCUPY A SEAT WHEN ADULTS ARE STANDING.

ANY PERSON WILFULLY DAMAGING THIS VEHICLE WILL BE PROSECUTED.

THE PLAYING OF RADIOS OR OTHER INSTRUMENTS CAUSING ANNOYANCE TO PASSENGERS IS PROHIBITED.

PLEASE KEEP THE PLATFORM CLEAR.

DO NOT DISTRACT THE DRIVER'S ATTENTION WHILST THE VEHICLE IS IN MOTION.

PASSENGERS BOARDING OR ALIGHTING WHILST THE VEHICLE IS IN MOTION DO SO AT THEIR OWN RISK.

These two photographs were produced for South Wales Transport to celebrate 75 years of service to the public. The single decker is based on AEC equipment, it has a Reliance chassis (probably one of if not the best ever built) with rather utilitarian Marshall of Cambridge bodywork. Delivered in 1962, 846 like her three sisters had left the fleet by 1974.

Not perhaps the most elegant of bodies, nonetheless No. 1212 and her four sisters had a seating capacity of 72 with standard length (30 ft) Park Royal bodywork. This was a unitary body with AEC running gear, intended to be a provincial version of the London Routemaster. The main advantage was the ease with which passengers could board such a lowheight body. Completed 1960, they were sold to a Yorkshire operator in 1969.

Plaxton Panorama bodywork on a rear-engined Daimler shows the magnificent area of glass that made coaching that much less claustrophobic.

SHEFFIELD TRANSPORT DEPARTMENT

WE HAVE A NUMBER OF

VACANCIES

FOR MEN WITH HEAVY VEHICLE EXPERIENCE TO TRAIN AS

BUS DRIVERS

- **GUARANTEED WEEK**
- **OPPORTUNITIES FOR OVERTIME**
- **FREE UNIFORM**
- **FREE TRAVEL TO AND FROM WORK**
- **SICKNESS ALLOWANCES**
- **EXCELLENT CANTEEN FACILITIES**

If you think YOU could meet our requirements, please apply personally or by telephone (78111) to the Personnel Office, Division Street.

Monday to Friday .. *9.0 a.m. to 5.0 p.m*
Saturday .. .. *9.0 am. to 11.30 a.m.*

This advertisement for drivers appeared in the May 1963 timetable issued by the Sheffied Transport & Joint Omnibus Committee.

Service Nos. 36, 36A — DERBY AND LOUGHBOROUGH
Service Nos. 625, 626 — DERBY AND LEICESTER VIA LOUGHBOROUGH

Service Nos. ...	625	36 F	626	36 F	626	36A A MFO	36A A TWTh	36 F	625	625 Su	625 S	626	36	625 Su	625 S	36	625	36
	a.m	a.m	p.m	p.m	p.m	p.m	p.m	p.m	p.m	a.m	p.m	p.m	p.m	p.m	p.m	p.m	p.m	p.m
DERBY (Bus Station)	8 50	1015	1250	3 32	4 45	5 0	5 30	7 27	8 55	1015	1230	1250	3 32	4 30	5 0	7 27	8 55	1040
Derby (Midland Station)	8 53	1018	1253	3 35	4 48	5 3	5 33	7 30	8 58	1018	1233	1253	3 35	4 33	5 3	7 30	8 58	1043
Derby (R.R.Works, Nightingale Rd.)	—	—	—	—	—	5 6	5 36	—	—	—	—	—	—	—	—	—	—	—
Alvaston (Coronation Avenue)	9 3	1028	1 3	3 45	4 58	5 13	5 43	7 40	9 8	1028	1243	1 3	3 45	4 43	5 13	7 40	9 8	1053
Aston Lane End	9 7	1032	1 7	3 49	5 3	5 17	5 47	7 44	9 12	1032	1247	1 7	3 49	4 47	5 17	7 44	9 12	1057
Shardlow (Dog & Duck)	9 11	1036	1 11	3 53	5 7	5 21	5 51	7 48	9 16	1036	1251	1 11	3 53	4 51	5 21	7 48	9 16	11 1
Castle Donington Turn	9 15	1040	1 15	3 57	5 12	5 25	5 55	7 52	9 20	1040	1255	1 15	3 57	4 55	5 25	7 52	9 20	11 5
Castle Donington (Turk's Head)	—	1045	—	4 2	—	—	—	7 57	—	—	1045	—	—	4 2	—	7 57	—	1110
Castle Donington (Moira Dale)	—	1047	—	4 4	—	—	—	7 59	—	—	1047	—	—	4 4	—	7 59	—	1112
Hemington	—	1049	—	4 6	—	—	—	8 1	—	—	1049	—	—	4 6	—	8 1	—	1114
Lockington	—	1051	—	4 8	—	—	—	8 3	—	—	1051	—	—	4 8	—	8 3	—	1116
Kegworth (Post Office)	9 22	1057	1 22	4 14	5 20	5 32	6 2	8 9	9 27	1057	1 2	1 22	4 14	5 2	5 32	8 9	9 27	1122
Hathern (Green)	9 30	11 5	1 30	4 22	5 29	5 40	6 10	8 17	9 35	11 5	1 10	1 30	4 22	5 10	5 40	8 17	9 35	1130
Loughborough (The Rushes)	9 37	1112	1 37	4 29	5 36	5 47	6 17	8 24	9 42	1112	1 17	1 37	4 29	5 17	5 47	8 24	9 42	1137
Loughborough (Lemyngton Street)	9 40	—	1 40	—	5 40	—	—	—	9 45	1115	1 20	1 40	—	5 20	5 50	—	9 45	—
Quorn (Post Office)	9 50	—	1 50	—	5 50	—	—	—	9 55	1125	1 30	1 50	—	5 30	6 0	—	9 55	—
Mountsorrel (Green)	9 58	—	1 58	—	5 58	—	—	—	10 3	1133	1 38	1 58	—	5 38	6 8	—	10 3	—
Rothley (Green)	10 5	—	2 5	—	6 5	—	—	—	10 10	1140	1 45	2 5	—	5 45	6 15	—	10 10	—
Birstall (Sibsons' Lane Corner)	1012	—	2 12	—	6 12	—	—	—	1017	1147	1 52	2 12	—	5 52	6 22	—	1017	—
Leicester (St.Margaret's Bus Station)	1027	—	2 27	—	6 27	—	—	—	1032	12 2	2 7	2 27	—	6 7	6 37	—	1032	—
LEICESTER (Southgate St. Bus Stn.)	1031	—	2 31	—	6 31	—	—	—	1036	12 6	2 11	2 31	—	6 11	6 41	—	1036	—

Service Nos. 36, 36A — LOUGHBOROUGH AND DERBY
Service Nos. 625, 626 — LEICESTER AND DERBY VIA LOUGHBOROUGH

Service No. ...	36A B	36	625	36 F	625	36 F	36 B	626	625 S	36 Su	626 †	625 S Su	36	626 †	36	625 Su	625 S	625 Su	625 S
	a.m	a.m	a.m	p.m	p.m	p.m	p.m	p.m	a.m	a.m	a.m	p.m	p.m	p.m	p.m	p.m	p.m	p.m	p.m
LEICESTER (Southgate St. Bus Stn.)	—	—	9 26	—	2 36	—	—	6 36	8 16	—	9 36	1026	—	2 36	—	6 36	6 46	8 36	8 41
Leicester (St. Margaret's Bus Station)	—	—	9 30	—	2 40	—	—	6 40	8 20	—	9 40	1030	—	2 40	—	6 40	6 50	8 40	8 45
Birstall (Sibsons' Lane Corner)	—	—	9 45	—	2 55	—	—	6 55	8 35	—	9 55	1045	—	2 55	—	6 55	7 5	8 55	9 0
Rothley (Green)	—	—	9 52	—	3 2	—	—	7	8 42	—	10 2	1052	—	3 2	—	7	7 12	9 2	9 7
Mountsorrel (Green)	—	—	9 59	—	3 9	—	—	7 9	8 49	—	10 9	1059	—	3 9	—	7 9	7 19	9 9	9 14
Quorn (Post Office)	—	—	10 7	—	3 17	—	—	7 17	8 57	—	1017	11 7	—	3 17	—	7 17	7 27	9 17	9 22
Loughborough (Swan Street)	—	—	1017	—	3 27	—	—	7 27	9 7	—	1027	1117	—	3 27	—	7 27	7 37	9 27	9 32
Loughborough (The Rushes)	6 55	9 10	1020	1 45	3 30	5 45	6 30	7 30	9 10	9 10	1030	1120	1 45	3 30	5 45	7 30	7 40	9 40	9 40
Hathern (Green)	7 2	9 17	1027	1 52	3 37	5 52	6 37	7 37	9 17	9 17	1037	1127	1 52	3 37	5 52	7 37	7 47	9 47	9 47
Kegworth (Post Office)	7 10	9 25	1035	2 0	3 45	6 0	6 45	7 45	9 25	9 25	1045	1135	2 0	3 45	6 0	7 45	7 55	9 55	9 55
Lockington	—	9 31	—	2 6	—	6 6	—	—	9 31	9 31	—	—	2 6	—	6 6	—	—	10 1	10 1
Hemington	—	9 33	—	2 8	—	6 8	—	—	9 33	9 33	—	—	2 8	—	6 8	—	—	10 3	10 3
Castle Donington (Moira Dale)	—	9 35	—	2 10	—	6 10	—	—	9 35	9 35	—	—	2 10	—	6 10	—	—	10 5	10 5
Castle Donington (Turk's Head)	—	9 37	—	2 12	—	6 12	—	—	9 37	9 37	—	—	2 12	—	6·12	—	—	10 7	10 7
Castle Donington Turn	7 17	9 42	1040	2 17	3 50	6 17	6 50	7 50	9 42	9 42	1052	1142	2 17	3 52	6 17	7 52	8 2	1012	1012
Shardlow (Dog & Duck)	7 21	9 46	1046	2 21	3 56	6 21	6 56	7 56	9 46	9 46	1056	1146	2 21	3 56	6 21	7 56	8 6	1016	1016
Aston Lane End	7 25	9 50	1050	2 25	4 0	6 25	7 0	8 0	9 50	9 50	11 0	1150	2 25	4 0	6 25	8 0	8 10	1020	1020
Alvaston (Coronation Avenue)	7 29	9 54	1054	2 29	4 4	6 29	7 4	8 4	9 54	9 54	11 4	1154	2 29	4 4	6 29	8 4	8 14	1024	1024
Derby (R.R.Works, Nightingale Rd.)	7 36	—	—	—	—	—	—	—	—	—	—	—	—	—	—	—	—	—	—
Derby (Midland Station)	7 39	10 4	11 4	2 39	4 14	6 39	7 14	8 14	10 4	10 4	1114	12 4	2 39	4 14	6 39	8 14	8 24	1034	1034
DERBY (Bus Station)	7 42	10 7	11 7	2 42	4 17	6 42	7 17	8 17	10 7	10 7	1117	12 7	2 42	4 17	6 42	8 17	8 27	1037	1037

Service No. 626 operates via Birstall Village (except 2.36 p.m. ex Leicester on Sundays).

† On these journeys no passengers will be picked up between Hathern and Kegworth for setting down between Hathern and Kegworth (except 2.36 p.m. ex Leicester on Sundays).

A On these journeys no passengers will be picked up nearer to Loughborough than Castle Donington Turn.

B On these journeys no passengers will be set down nearer to Loughborough than Castle Donington Turn.

TRENT

1913-1963 GOLDEN JUBILEE YEAR

TIMETABLE

FOR ALL ROUTES
FROM APRIL 14TH 1963 UNTIL FURTHER NOTICE

9D.

One of the oddities about the Nottingham-Derby axis was the intense loyalty of passengers to 'their' operator. They had a fairly healthy choice from the mid-1930s with the various corporation fleets, Blue Bus of Willington, Barton, Trent Motor Traction Company and other companies, all competing for their custom. From our angle, working for a small firm on the edge of the TMT area, the only use we had for British Electric Traction companies (of which Trent was one) was their cast-off vehicles kept us in business! But Trent had spread their tentacles widely with Manchester, Blackpool, Glasgow, Edinburgh, London, Lowestoft, Cromer, Lincoln, Cleethorpes and Birmingham among the destinations served daily. Their other great advantage was that their management were professionals to their very bones and although BET training, via other companies in the group, made them dry and uncomfortable bedfellows it may have been better for passengers than the often eccentric and (alas) maintenance-free approach of the small fry. Their timetables were magnificent examples of their kind.

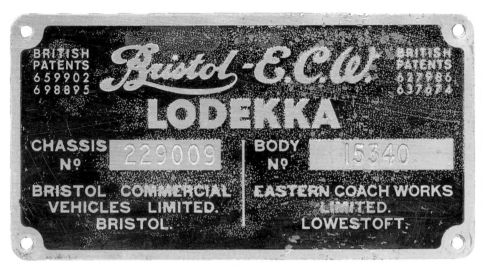

The co-operation between Bristol and Eastern Coach Works included their vehicles having joint builders plates. FLF6G number AA 24 was delivered 1965 to Scottish Omnibuses, the group name at that time for Eastern Scottish, Baxters Bus Service and Stark's Motor Services. This was part of the old Scottish Motor Traction Company (SMT), itself one-time owned by the LMS and LNE Railways, and in effect 'the' operator in Scotland. FLF6G was a type of Bristol Lodekka with certain distinctive features. Flat floor, Long chassis, Front entrance, 6-cylindered Gardner engine; Scottish Omnibuses rather specialized in a 31 ft variant.

De Luxe Coach Services commenced operations in 1927 as Evans Brothers based at a pub, the Black Horse Inn at Atherstone, moving in 1931 to their garage at Mancetter, Warwickshire. A rather handsome colour scheme of red, white and black graced their vehicles of which 543 OHU, a Bristol Lodekka FLF6B ex-Bristol Omnibus, new in 1963 as No. C.7098, was a member for a while. The licence, without which no PSV could be operated, is a rare survivor and a rarely seen aspect of bus work. Vastly simplified, any Public Service Vehicle has to be tested annually on or before the first anniversary of its registration.

The test makes a car MOT pale into insignificance and carried out conscientiously means that at the time of the examination the vehicle is fit for its intended duty in every respect. Such a little piece of paper for all that! And yet 'travellers' require neither driving licence, MOT or any other documentation - are they so much safer than a skilled driver and enthusiastic operator?

May 1969. There were many examples of railway companies operating buses, but until recently very few of bus companies operating railways! Saltburn Motor Services was possibly unique in that it owned and operated a miniature railway in the beach-side park at the foot of this hill. Railways aside, it is quite a spectacular section of this route.
Keith Turns

One of the more charming idiosyncrasies of old-style licensing. In July 1969 Scarlet Band, with Trimdon Motor Services and Gillett's in the distance, works its service out of New Elvet in Durham City. This operated only on Gala Day but was under a special licence acquired annually for the one day. Eventually, by the 1980s, United Automobile Services claimed this old-established service was unnecessary and renewal was refused. Durham lost another operator.
Keith Turns

In the end all bus work has to meet certain financial parameters. Until recently, there were a good number of operators who ran their vehicles almost as a hobby; so much so that any accountant who looked at the figures would suffer heart palpitations. Improbably in the 1960s there was a company who not only did not have a full-time secretary (she drove the school bus but they did not have an answerphone) and another who, when the proprietor and his daughter went on holiday, left the whole concern in the hands of a pleasant but at best semi-literate driver, just because they had done so for 30 years. And we drivers all knew the nice little tour office girls who never seemed to quite sort out getting the right passengers in the right seats on the right bus.

TELEPHONE
CONSETT
282 3 LINES

Venture
Transport
COMPANY (NEWCASTLE) LIMITED

DIRECTORS
G. R. HARRISON (Secretary)
W. T. RICHARDSON
W. C. REED
E. REED
E. REED
GENERAL MANAGER
L. GRAHAM, A. M. Inst. T.

16-17 PRINCES STREET · CONSETT · CO. DURHAM

No. 137 in the Venture Transport Company (Newcastle) Ltd fleet GPT 965 was a 1947 Daimler CVD 6 with a conservatively styled Willowbrook 35-seat body. It was sold in 1961 to Jim Batty, who had started business in 1946 when he bought John Robson's services in the Wansbeck Valley, Northumberland for £5,000. The goodwill of three bus services on two licences was rated at £3,640, while the balance was for three buses. GPT 965 was Jim Batty's eleventh vehicle, only two of which had been new. Venture, once the largest independent operator in County Durham, sold out to the National Bus Company in 1970.

VENTURE TRANSPORT CO. (NCLE) LTD.

MONTH SEPTEMBER, 1961.

PCM

ROUTE		£	s	d	PENCE	MILES	FROM
CONSETT SHOTLEY NCLE	11	7041	13	10½	1690006	61851	27.3
CONTRACT TICKETS							
HEXHAM	2	13	15	3½	3303	344	9.6
WHITTONSTALL	2	35	5	5	8465	922	9.1
BLANCHLAND	3	237	14	0½	57048	4273	13.3
HOSPITAL NEWCASTLE	11	160	9	3	38511	798	48.2
TEMPLETOWN	6	98	12	10½	23674	635	37.2
BRIDGEHILL	4	939	11	0½	225492	4710	47.8
HAT & FEATHER	7	778	17	10	186934	5826	32.0
CONSETT MED. NEWCASTLE	52	2658	3	3	637959	31266	20.4
CONTRACT TICKETS							
CROOKHALL	8	310	6	5	74477	2408	30.9
C. I. C. CHOPWELL		628	16	8	150920	4556	33.1
CHOPWELL CONSETT	30	1220	1	10½	292822	10.386	28.1
C. I. C. BRIDGEHILL		135	4	5	32453	641	50.6
LONGBENTON	00	301	16	10½	72442	2848	25.4
ELM PARK	9	389	5	2	93422	2554	36.5
OAKDALE	10						
HIGH WESTWOOD	12	401	12	7	96391	3491	27.6
C. I. C. ALLENDALE		224	16	3½	53955	1328	35.3
C. I. C. LEADGATE		10	1	11¼	2423	162	14.9
WINLATON MILL NCLE.	66	201	0	10	48250	2005	24.0
WIN. MILL WINLATON SCH.		17	16	0½	4272	91	46.9
STANHOPE	14	209	5	4½	50224	2129	23.5
BROOMS CHURCH							
CHOPWELL LEADGATE	13	733	11	3½	176055	8965	19.6
CHOPWELL NCLE. RYTON	22	3851	18	3½	924459	32561	28.3
CONSTRACT TICKETS							
CHOPWELL NCLE ROWLANDS GILL	35	4700	15	3	1128183	34826	32.3
CONTRACT TICKETS							
FOLLY NEWCASTLE	44	1365	7	0½	327684	17102	19.1
HEDLEY	77	144	8	1½	34657	1291	26.8
SOUTH WYLAM	55	350	5	1½	84061	3162	26.5
CHOPWELL PRUDHOE	15	327	16	8½	78680	4755	16.5
HIGH SPEN NEWBURN	17	351	12	1	84385	3268	25.8
CHOPWELL I. C. I.	16	56	1	11	13463	485	27.7
MINERS	0	64	2	5½	15389	817	18.8
C & E STANLEY	25 31	2824	0	8	677768	22718	29.8

The Venture accounts sheet is an unusual survivor and shows how income could vary from route to route; no decimals as, given the devaluation of the pound, the figures are comparative only. The final column shows earnings per mile (pence ÷ miles).

To some extent, most people have a perceived opinion of buses - cold, dank and upstairs streaming with
yellow nicotine-enhanced condensation. In conditions like those shown here, this is not too far off! But on a
summer's evening where better for a courting couple to go? Hull 1944 Guy Arab II with later NCME body
awaits departure.

Wolverhampton Guy Arab IV with MCCW bodywork, one of a batch of 50 supplied between 1959 and 1961,
waiting departure from Walsall.

It is surprisingly hard to find truly 'just about awake' photographs of buses. The North Western Road Car Company was partly railway owned (LMS 30 per cent LNER 15 per cent) but run as a wholly independent concern with the staff showing an amazing degree of loyalty to their company. Fleet No. 792 (LDB 792) was a Willowbrook of Loughborough-bodied Leyland Tiger Cub delivered 1960 and having 43 dual purpose (bus/coach) seats. The 0. 350 engine used in these was notorious for making the sparrows cough early in the day; the running boy will shortly join their chorus. Painted in red, black and cream the smartness of this bus hides the vast mileage they covered. No. 646, behind, is another Tiger Cub but with 'pure' basic bus bodywork by MCW built 1956. However from time to time they would appear on the Manchester-Scarborough service, when the rear pairs of seats had to be reserved for luggage, there being no boot - and a right caper that was for the driver and conductor alike.

Bedlington & District Luxury Coaches of Ashington, Northumberland, ran a complex series of services to and from the local villages and coal mines and other industries. Although the days of wooden-slatted seats for miners' use had gone (as indeed had the days of poaching with Bedlington terriers) contract prices ensured the company was always on the lookout for bargains. Four out of 25 or so vehicles in use at any one time are shown. The three double-deckers are all ex-London Transport (left to right, RT 600, RT 4586 and RT 3146) but the flat-topped AEC Regent V 281 DWN is a real rarity, the Roe body (seating 37) being built in 1962 to lo-lo height (8 ft 11 in.) for use by the South Wales Transport Co. on a restricted clearance route in the Llanelly docks area; the eight of this class were the only single deck Regent V buses to operate in the United Kingdom. Withdrawn in 1972 one (282 DWN) survives in the care of the Welsh Industrial and Maritime Museum.

table 4   TOLLESBURY · MALDON

weekdays

	NS	NS			S	NS☆	●	✶.	✶	✶			NS●
	am	am	am	am	am	am	am	pm	pm	pm	pm	pm	pm
TOLLESBURY square............	6 55	7 25	8 20	9 30	....	..	....	....	....	....	1 45	....	....
TOLLESHUNT D'ARCY lion........	7 00	7 31	8 26	9 36	....	..	....	....	....	....	1 51	....	....
TOLLESHUNT MAJOR lanes garage.	....	....	....	9 42	....	....	....	....	....	....	1 57	....	....
LITTLE TOTHAM pennys brook....	....	....	....	9 46	....	....	....	....	....	....	2 01	....	....
LITTLE TOTHAM post office.....	....	....	....	9 48	....	....	....	....	....	....	2 03	....	....
LITTLE TOTHAM renters corner..	....	....	....	9 50	....	....	....	....	....	....	2 05	....	....
GOLDHANGER rectory corner.....	7 08	7 39	8 34	9 55	....	....	....	....	....	....	2 10	....	....
GOLDHANGER square.............	7 10	....	8 36	9 57	1035	....	....	....	....	....	2 12	3 00	....
OSEA ROAD.....................	7 14	7 43	8 40	1001	1039	....	....	....	....	....	2 16	3 04	....
MILL BEACH hotel..............	7 16	7 45	8 42	1003	1041	1045	....	1130	1230	1 30	2 18	3 06	....
HEYBRIDGE BASIN...............	....	....	8 45	....	....	1048	1130	....	....	....	....	3 09	3 48
TOLLGATE......................	7 18	7 47	8 47	1005	1043	1050	1132	1132	1232	1 32	2 20	3 11	3 50
HEYBRIDGE street..............	7 21	7 50	8 52	1008	1046	1053	1135	1135	1235	1 35	2 23	3 16	3 53
MALDON east station road......	7 23	....	8 54	1010	1048	1055	1137	1137	1237	1 37	2 25	3 18	3 55
MALDON victoria road..........	....	....	8 57	1012	1050	1057	1139	1139	1239	1 39	2 27	3 21	3 57

	✶	✶	MTTh	WFS	✶	NS☆	NS	S	S	W☽
	pm	pm	pm	pm	pm	pm	pm	pm	pm	pm
TOLLESBURY square............	....	....	5 15	5 15	...	7 00	7 00	....	....	9 45
TOLLESHUNT D'ARCY lion........	....	....	5 21	5 21	....	7 06	7 06	....	....	9 51
TOLLESHUNT MAJOR lanes garage.	....	....	....	5 27	....	....	7 12	....	....	....
LITTLE TOTHAM pennys brook....	....	....	....	5 31	....	....	7 16	....	....	....
LITTLE TOTHAM post office.....	....	....	....	5 33	....	....	7 18	....	....	....
LITTLE TOTHAM renters corner..	....	....	....	5 35	....	....	7 21	....	....	....
GOLDHANGER rectory corner.....	....	....	5 29	5 40	....	7 14	7 26	....	....	9 59
GOLDHANGER square.............	....	....	5 31 s	5 42	....	7 16	7 28	....	8 30	1001
OSEA ROAD.....................	....	....	5 35	5 46	....	7 20	7 32	....	8 34	1005
MILL BEACH hotel..............	3 48	4 30	5 37	5 48	6 30	7 22	7 34	....	8 36	1007
HEYBRIDGE BASIN...............	....	....	....	....	....	....	....	....	8 39	....
TOLLGATE......................	3 50	4 32	5 39	5 51	6 32	7 24	7 36	....	8 41	1009
HEYBRIDGE street..............	3 53	4 35	5 42	5 53	6 35	7 27	7 39	....	8 44	1012
MALDON east station road......	3 55	4 37	5 44	5 55	6 37	7 29	7 41	....	8 46	1014
MALDON victoria road..........	3 57	4 39	5 46	5 57	6 39	7 31	7 43	....	8 48	1016

efd f8

Osborne's of Tollesbury commenced operating motorbuses in 1919. This timetable is dated 1968 and, apart from showing a remarkably extensive service is particularly of note for the post-10.30 departures whose strange codes indicate 'w' - Wednesdays only, the 'half-moon' - August only, and the 'maze' that this bus 'awaits conclusion of cinema'. The 's' tells us this runs every Saturday throughout the year. Around this time the bus was driven (without a conductor) by Jim Osborne, but in later years coaches returning from private hire would be diverted *en route* to their base to carry out this run.

OSBORNE'S

OFFICIAL BUS

TIMETABLES

1968

h b c publication

agd 117

6d

EX 6326 'The Felix' was a 1949 Duple-bodied Bedford OB coach, purchased from Felix Coaches, Great Yarmouth 1955 and withdrawn nine years later. She is standing at the then Maldon Terminus, Warwick Arms, Victoria Road. Photographed 31st July, 1960.

G.R. Mills

Standing at New Road, Tollesbury, ready washed, swept and refuelled for a Sunday service JNK 143 was two years older, purchased 1958 and remained in service until 1965. As Duple 'Vista' bodied OBs tended to look alike the three portholes on the bonnet side must have been an attempt to personalise the vehicle. Photographed 14th November, 1964.

G.R. Mills

Of late there has been much demand for improvements in school buses; but this particular clarion call has been echoing in the ears of operators for, to my knowledge, 40 years or more. Ideally what parents want is a cross between a Volvo Estate and a Rolls Royce to be provided individually for each child. Too often what they are willing to pay for is a tired 'contract motor' seating 53+. But AYT 224B was once a school bus and she was photographed in a layby on the 7th May, 1993. The notice in the windscreen stated she was waiting parts and not abandoned. The location is Pillerton Priors on the A422 near Stratford. The chassis is BMC, the bodywork Martin Walter (Dormobile).

A rather intriguing contrast at Crawley, Sussex, between the coach SPK 202W, a London Country Bus Services AEC Reliance 6U3ZR with Plaxton Panorama Elite III bodywork containing 49 coach seats whose antimacassors with National 'double arrow' logo are visible through the windscreen, and the bus-bodied PWN 702H. An AEC Swift 2MP2R with Willowbrook twin-door 48-seat bodywork, this vehicle was new to South Wales Transport in 1969 but joined London Country two years later. Alas, the Sun public house in the left background was demolished mid-1996 to make way for yet another bypass.

Restoration of service to the remote fastnesses of Lunedale. Television records for posterity the opening of a school service to ordinary passengers in March 1977, the first service since Darlington Triumph withdrew post-war. The initiative came from the County Planning Department which had a representative on the bus. He was NOT interviewed; after all, Councils have to have a bad name! Both the swirling mist and the vehicle (Plaxton-bodied Bedford) typified time and place. Shown here operated by Teesdale Coach Services.   *Keith Turns*

All classes of vehicles serving the public have been regarded as useful mobile bill-boards for many centuries whether market waggons, mail coaches or express trains and, emulating their horse-drawn predecessors, it was not long before buses and coaches became festooned with advertising. The most unthinking aspect of this has always been the posting of handbills inside windows thus obstructing the passenger's view. At best they only irritate but can, especially at night on driver only-operated buses, lead to travellers unfamiliar with the route missing their stops. Exterior advertising has varied from the discreet to the garish, from the informative to grotesque. Three out of four vehicles shown here are apparently of a similar manufacturer's combination but differ greatly. Jubilee Garage's advertisement is on FFR 173S; Burnley & Pendle fleet No. 173, new in 1978 with an Eastern Coach Works (ECW) 74-seat body on a Bristol VRT chassis powered by the classic Gardner 6LXB diesel engine.

Colchester is the logical place to advertise the *Essex County Standard* and here the all-over artistry somewhat overpowers the destination blind within the ECW 74-seat body, this time on a Leyland Atlantean AN 68 A/IR chassis.

This fine example of graphic art was multi-coloured on a yellow background and was quite striking, the hand pre-dating the Lottery one of today! No. 193, then in the fleet of Southampton City Transport, has an Atlantean chassis identical to that of Colchester but graced with rather more distinctive East Lancs 76-seat bodywork. The trainer behind, No. 920, leaves no doubt what its duties are.

Although this Bristol is advertising 'in house' holidays and advises us that these can be booked at Swansea, Neath, Port Talbot, Llanelli, Gorseinon, Morriston and Skewen, the odd thing is why in that most Welsh part of Wales no part of the advertisement is in Welsh. The vehicle VTH 940T is No. 940 in the South Wales Transport Company's ownership. Another Bristol VRT, albeit Leyland engined, once again she carries an ECW 74-seat body.

Seen passing the then new Birmingham Snow Hill station (the greenhouse to the left of the coach), this beautifully maintained Plaxton-bodied Bristol was in use by the John Lewis Partnership for staff transport purposes.   *Daniel Hill Photography*

For some years shuttle services to and from the local supermarket have been operated often with a subsidy from the store, giving either free or reduced rate travel. One, Fine Fare, offered a refund on fares on production of a till receipt. Too often this proved to be only for the sale of a bag of sugar (itself a 'loss leader') and the contract was summarily cancelled almost without notice. Monkspath is a suburb of Solihull in the West Midlands and the vehicle a Plaxton-bodied Bedford built 1976.   *Gideon Graphics*

Beamish Rally September 1979. Batty of Morpeth, on the left, is about to deprive Calvary Coaches, on the right, of the Brian Sharpe Trophy. It is interesting that TWO operators in the County Durham area were religiously committed to the extent of naming their fleets especially; Calvary Coaches of evident evangelical persuasion and Stella Maris clearly Roman Catholic. Both vehicles are, however, alike in their origins – Duple-bodied Bedford OBs.   *Keith Turns*

One of the successes of the public transport team of a Council. Trimdon Motor Services extended its 236 route (Hartlepool to Sedgefield) round in a loop on Summer Sundays to serve Hardwick Hall Country Park. Here, in July 1976, TMS loads passengers otherwise unable to use a park whose upkeep they have paid for through their taxes.   *Keith Turns*

With hindsight we can see what a marvellous, if flawed, dream the Leyland National single-deck bus was in 1968. Much new technology was incorporated and its assembly was entrusted to a purpose-built factory built where, hitherto, industry was almost unknown, at Workington, Cumbria. Designed as a modular structure (rather akin to a submarine) one had a front and a back-cum-powerpak with sections as required in the middle. One result of this was that the vehicle had - has where still running - immense rollover strength but to allay fears over its crushability Leyland undertook a series of impact tests. At the time such tests were almost unknown within the PSV industry mainly as crash testing was a bit pointless with just a chassis, and bodybuilders could not afford to (as they saw it) wantonly destroy a new vehicle. The 'wall' is an immovable concrete block and the photographs show the moment of impact at 20 mph. The front module, including the driver's space has moved back as a unit while windows fitted to bays 3, 4 and 5 have stayed intact.

(All) British Leyland

The Leyland National was conceived as an 'all things to all men' machine with a possible assembly figure at Workington of 2,000 units per year. In 1967 Leyland calculated that the UK market could absorb 3,000 full-sized single-deck buses per annum but with only 10,000 such vehicles running in the UK then the National had to be capable of replacing most if not all the double-deck fleet as well. Even then, given a planned 10 year life their run at maximum production was never going to be for long. Worse, there was to be a swing against single-deckers between the planning date, 1968, and delivery of the first production vehicles in 1972. Within a year some awareness of possible failure concentrated minds wonderfully on the possibilities of varying the interior, while using a semi-standard bus shell. The Business Commuter was well before its time and had it been adopted by outside management personnel could have frightened the socks off British Rail. Sadly, years later what we know as executive coaches were and are in demand, but this demand is met by imported vehicles. Eight luxury seats were fitted each with a communication console, while it was intended that a secretary would be available at her 'work station'. At the rear was a lounge/conference area with perimeter seating for 12 and a small galley. Seatbelts were fitted although it was always envisaged that the passengers would be as free to wander as on a train. Rather surprisingly no toilet facilities were incorporated although full air conditioning was built-in - unlike the standard National 1 which had only cold feet/hot head inducing 'warm air curtains'. Eventually registered UTJ 595M this rather special vehicle was retained by Leyland as a mobile hospitality suite which purpose it performed well, although still with the characteristic National engine rasp, and rather pleasingly was handed to the British Commercial Vehicle Museum in 1987.

(All) British Leyland

South Yorkshire PTE was variously praised for its low fares, and cursed for causing high household and business rates by virtue of the subsidies paid. However, its buses, if not as smart as the old Sheffield fleets, were tidy and well maintained. No. 828 is a Daimler Fleetline with ECW bodywork delivered 1987.

Lancaster City Transport, incorporated the former Morecambe & Heysham Corporation fleet into its own but was, until forced out of business, a fine example of a tightly run bus fleet. Here two new arrivals ex-Greater Manchester PTE are seen in the garage at Morecambe. Both are Leyland Atlanteans and both have MCW bodywork but there are interesting detail differences.

The Metro-Cammell-Weymann Metrobus was a success story of the 1970s, mainly at the cost of British Leyland who seemed to suffer from policy confusion. The forerunner of the Metrobus was the Scania-powered Metropolitan, but for its successor MCW offered a choice of Gardner or Rolls~Royce engines. Unusually although the Metrobus always gave the impression of being an integral (chassis-less) design this was not so and a good percentage of their output was bodied by outside coachworks. The design proved to be a popular one, with London Transport taking a total of 1,440, although Greater Manchester Transport tended to buy more of a mixture of chassis, only 90 Metrobuses entering service. The original intention was that, like the National, the Metrobus would only be available in one model, but this plan was overcome by marketing factors; the two vehicles shown indicate some of the variety produced. Notwithstanding the introduction of the Metrorider minibus, the Mk II Metrobus and the Metroliner coach, MCW fell foul of political pressures and production ceased in 1988.   *Metro-Cammell-Weyman Ltd*

Right: United's 416 DCD (subsequently re-registered to PRX 190B) was a Leyland PD3 fitted with a convertible (detachable) roof when built in 1964 for Southdown, but is seen here following an inter-National Bus transfer at Scarborough. It is now preserved as are many of this type.

Above: TCD 377J (Crosville HCG 907) was a 1970 Daimler Fleetline with Northern Counties bodywork and is seen here operating to Prestatyn on a line service; most of the passengers look frozen.

Right: Moving away from the seaside, country and town tours are also in vogue. Rossendale Transport Ltd have basically inter-urban routes passing, however, through attractive Lancashire countryside. VTD 702T is a Leyland Atlantean with East Lancs 75-seat bodywork.

New in the sunshine of 1978, this MCW Metrobus for London Transport was one of 300 fitted with Voith Diwa D851 fully automatic bus transmissions which were destined for service with both LT and the West Midlands PTE.
Voith Engineering Ltd

The biggest 'what if' in the midi-bus world must lie in the question: 'What if Bedford had not suffered from indecision over the future of their JJL?' This unregistered prototype was photographed on 1st April, 1979 to demonstrate the ease of entry with a low step height and wide door opening. Even today these would be plus-points and the body design still looks modern. The outline was conceived by Marshall's of Cambridge by 1974, reworked by Bedford and appeared at the 1976 Commercial Motor Show. By 1979 around 150 had been ordered but only the four demonstrators were sold, the project being effectively dead by 1985.
Vauxhall Motors Ltd

Posed, perhaps, but classically Birmingham City Transport regardless of the newly painted West Midlands PTE logo on the side. This was a time of modestly concealed radiators and of less concealling skirts, but No. 2621, a Guy Arab IV with that most British of engines the Gardner 6 LW, was delivered in 1951, passed to the PTE in 1969, lasted until 1975, and is seen in her immaculate livery of khaki roof, deep blue and cream.

Lonely and waiting her fate 4070 JW, ex-No. 70N in the Wolverhampton Corporation fleet, was an example of that most unhappy of designs, the Wulfrunian. Guy Motors lacked the resources to develop a rear-engined chassis to rival the Leyland Atlantean but tried to manufacture a state-of-the art 'normal' vehicle, with a massive Gardner diesel canted over into the driver's space, in order to allow space for a forward entrance plus full air suspension and disc brakes all round. This combination was all too much for most operators who still regarded leaf springs, drum brakes and a conductor as the 'right' way of doing things! Purchased in 1961 with East Lancs bodywork as one of 137 Wulfrunians built, 70N was out of use half her life before going for scrap in 1972.

Obviously, the engine of a bus is one of the most important aspects, but it is also one of the least seen. ANH 194 is a preserved ex-Northampton Daimler CVG 6 bus built in 1947. The engine is a normally aspirated Gardner 6 LW developing 102 bhp at 1,700 rpm of a design that first entered service in 1931 and was not finally withdrawn from the market until 1974.

Another 'standard' Gardner engine series is the 6 LX. First introduced in 1958 and developing 150 bhp still at the relatively slow 1,700 rpm, this was available in upright, horizontal and marine guises. The subsequent 6 LXB variant (introduced 1966) broke all economy figures with a consumption of 0.328 lb/bhp/hr representing 40 per cent thermal efficiency. The horsepower available rose to 180, this rising with the 6 LXC to 201 hp at 1,920 rpm in 1978. Turbocharging arrived in 1981, with eventually 400-odd hp being available on tap.

Included in the problem areas of transverse rear-mounted engines are heat, access and both induction and exhaust noise. Obviously any diesel requires copious quantities of nice cold air but mostly gets already used smog, not dissimilar to that we breathe. Compared with a forward mounted engine the exhaust has to be stubby, and access for servicing is somewhat one sided. This 1974 view shows the then-new 'quiet pack' on a Mk3 Bristol WRT; particularly evident is the cooling air duct casting allowing this to be drawn from the mid-deck area where, theoretically, it is cleaner and the induction roar nullified.   *British Leyland*

JTV 48SE, No. 489 in the fleet of Nottingham City Transport, was a Leyland Atlantean PDR2/1 with MCW 76-seat bodywork, which ended its days in Gloucester as a school bus. The Atlantean was one of the first one-person-operated rear-engined double-deck vehicle designs and inevitably suffered from many problems, not the least that the driver up front was blissfully ignorant of what was happening to the engine at the back-end. During intensive city work heat from the rear brakes could combine with the engine's heat (exacerbated by a build up of road dirt and oil on the engine) and either make water hoses go soggy and crack or the engine oil overheat. On cooling the resultant vacuum would draw air into the system leading to air locks and a failed engine. On one occasion in 1992 the N45 service from Birmingham had three vehicle changes in 8 hours as the driver found his heaters to be u/s and cared enough to report the problem. At worst the engine would catch fire, the fan feeding in air to encourage a real fry-up! A 1967 bus, No. 485 is having her Leyland 11.1 litre engine pressure cleaned, prior to overhaul. Some indication of the then relatively new one-person-operation lies in the (sexist!) notice above the bustle: the lack of personal protection for the man holding the lance would not be tolerated today.

The first articulated buses in Britain were steamers before World War I and although a few were used during 1939-45 they were never really regarded as more than a stop gap. It is not really surprising then that when plans were laid to import new generation Bendi-buses into Britain, resistance was felt, not least from the licensing authorities who, it seems, doubted the ability of a British driver to handle them. One feels a hearty 'pshaw' was an apposite response. However, there was a very real belief then (and, alas, now) that 'our' double-deckers will be outlawed by the Common Market and we will have to use artic-buses sooner or later. Four examples are shown in these pages. The Leyland-DAB test bus was built by Leyland Motors' Danish subsidiary, DAB, although based on Saurer patents, with a Saurer engine, while the bodywork also drew heavily on Swiss knowledge, using the Alusuisse aluminium alloy designs, and ran as a demonstrator in 1977.

Leyland Motors

From the Leyland-DAB evolved this National bus lookalike on a Leyland-DAB chassis but using a Leyland engine, which entered service with the South Yorkshire PTE in Sheffield in September 1979. Unfortunately as Construction & Use Regulations had not been adapted to allow this and its sisters (five in all) to be licensed no fares could be charged, although a capacity of 120 allowed crowds to be shifted nearly as well as the despised trams Sheffield had dumped in 1960. Due to this and some trade union difficulties the service was withdrawn in 1981. However, subsequent changes to the C&U regulations has allowed Bendi-buses to become almost commonplace now.

CLM 346T was built by the German company MAN, who saw enough interest in the market to produce a right-hand drive variant on their already successful design. This bus was first demonstrated in 1978 and notwithstanding an operating unladen weight of near 13 tonnes could cope with 162 passengers. Alas, all but 70 would have had to stand, but CLM 346T served well enough as one of a batch of five sent to Sheffield to run alongside the Leyland offerings. After service with the South Yorkshire PTE, these five, reduced in capacity to 53 plus 67 in the trailer, passed from MAN's workshops in Swindon to Midland Red (North) operating in Chaserider colours, as Nos. 1801-1805.   *L. Simpson*

Earlier, in Sheffield, DAK 301V, one of the production batch of four which accompanied CLM shows her clearly continental derivation, the Goppel bodywork being quite different to that made in Britain at the time.

The Leyland National, as a vehicle, might have had a magnificent future not only as a bus, but a multi-purpose shell. This Lifeliner was one of many projects tried at Workington and first appeared at the 1974 Earls Court Show (this photograph was embargoed until 13th September) as a design for a mobile casualty and communications centre which could be rushed to the scene of a major accident, thus replacing the fleets of ambulances which try to get there and back to accident and emergency wards. Various modifications were made to the standard National, not least a high floor allowing oxygen, water and drainage tanks to be fitted as well as a variant on the air suspension that permitted each wheel to be adjusted individually, compensating for uneven ground. At the front provision was made for tractor haulage across country and for fitting to 'shore lines'. Cost of each unit was high and health authorities preferred to buy ordinary ambulances - but one wonders if this was the right decision? Perhaps so, as helicopters become more available. *British Leyland*

Bus stops used to vary in size, shape and colour throughout the country. This is no longer true except here and there where a dwindling band of survivors from yesteryear hang on. *Above:* Hednesford Bus Station., *Below left:* Stafford. *Below right:* Macclesfield

Above left: Sheffield.

Daniel Hill Photography

Above right: Wythall Bus Museum.

Left: Tie clip: South Yorkshire. Green and white on 'brass'.

Right: Jacket badge: Alder Valley Inspector. Red and blue on brass.

A photograph taken to show the new Evershed & Vignoles electronic destination indicator and route number display on this new Northern Counties-bodied Leyland Atlantean which it indisputably does, but it also highlights the distinctive City of Nottingham frontal design - one that at least puts the display where eyes automatically look. ARC 666T was one of 296 Atlanteans delivered over an eight year period.

Evershed & Vignoles

School buses are a provision often forced on local councils as few private operators can afford to have dedicated vehicles lying idle outside the hour or two twice a day they are utilized. Obviously any bus is better for rush hour traffic purposes than the stream of Mums arriving in their Volvo and Synergie vehicles. XHV 687T (Locomotors-bodied Bedford, Inner London EA), KMU 836P (Ford/Marshall, Waltham Forest BC) and MLB 116L (Bedford/Strachans, Lewisham BC) are examples of purpose-built non-PSV vehicles of particular ugliness, while the two unregistered ex-M0D buses, seen at a dealers, were both later destined for school work.

Above and right: Before VNB 170L became a playbus with the Shrewsbury-based Shropshire Playbus Association this was a perfectly normal Park Royal-bodied Atlantean in the fleet of Greater Manchester PTE, No. 7070 in a batch of 150 delivered in 1972. Obviously the interior is heavily modified and the emergency exit (*right*) is unusual. Photographed 1996 at a Kit Car Show.

In a panoramic view of the bus and coach world one continually finds 'might-have-beens'. Not all of these have died through any inherent fault of their own, but the sponsor may lose enthusiasm, run out of money, or just give up. Tracline 65 was an attempt to run a bus as a tram. Primary advantages are that almost any bus can be modified to suit,

installation costs are negligible, 25 per cent less road space is required compared to a normal bus, and unlike a 'bus lane' few cars will try to enter the trough while even fewer will park. And, most of all, when the bus comes out of the track it can run as a normal vehicle. The West Midlands PTE laid their experimental 600 metre-long line up the Lichfield Road to Short Heath, Birmingham, utilising the central reservation, which was once the line of a tramway, abandoned mainly as it was considered dangerous practice to load passengers in the centre of the road. WMPTE tried very hard to make the line work, even to the extent of installing new pelican crossings and fitting new phased traffic lights. The method of operation, reproduced from a leaflet of the time with the permission of Centro is described thus: 'The busway consists of twin track formed from concrete slab with steel guide rails. The bus enters the track from the ordinary roadway at the end. When entering the system all the driver has to do is steer the bus to bring the offside guide wheel into gentle contact with the leading guide rail. After a short distance the bus engages smoothly with the nearside guide rail and the bus's road wheels are located between the vertical steel guide rails. The special guidance system steers by means of horizontal rollers. These are in contact with the guide rails and are mounted on levers which directly steer the vehicle. The driver is free to concentrate on control of his vehicle's speed and ensure that he stops and pulls away smoothly at each passenger station'. In this photograph three out of 14 special Metrobuses can be seen being demonstrated in 1984. Although the line was not continued and the buses had their special equipment removed in less than five years they retained their larger than standard destination indicators and other minor fittings. Unique at the time of its inception, Tracline was the first guided busway to take double-deck vehicles and had WMPTE not been dissolved by government decree they might well still be leading the world.

City buses by their nature can only be box-shaped in order to get in the maximum number of passengers. However the packaging of the box is as important as their capacity. The West Midlands offering is a standard Metrobus, the London General a Leyland Titan.

This Bus must not be driven under any of the low Bridges listed in the Traffic Operators Handbook

(1) Windsor Road, Penarth.
(2) Nantgarw Road, Caerphilly.
Not to operate on routes –
28, 29, 36, 307/8, 315 – 318 & Caerphilly GKN

'If you are re-directed because of a sudden incident (e.g. by the police) take particular care keeping a look out for trees and overhead obstructions, particularly low bridges. The height of our double-deck buses is 14 ft 7 in. and the height of our single-deck buses is 10 ft 3 in. This information is the key to avoiding accidents involving low bridges. All low bridges are clearly marked with the maximum headroom for a vehicle passing underneath, so bear your height in mind when driving outside the City on private hire'. This warning was issued by Leicester City Transport in 1981. Elsewhere a sticker roughly in line with the driver's eyesight gave succinct information. The basic difference between low height and 'standard' vehicles is clearly apparent here. The red PMT vehicle (766 EVT) is a Leyland PDRI with 1959 Weymann 73-seat bodywork, while Wallasey No. 1 (FHF 451) is also a PDRI but with Metro-Cammell 77-seat bodywork. They were photographed together on the 12th August, 1980 at the Southport rally.   *Alan Robinson*

Brand new in 1981 and the new 26-seater MAN-VW midicoach has been tilted successfully to an angle of 35 degrees to meet UK PSV requirements. Based on a MAN-VW 8.136 MT chassis the body, manufactured by Reeve Burgess, includes tubular and folded steel sections with aluminium panelling and glass fibre front and rear panel mouldings. The large window area is glazed with tinted glass and the interior incorporates a forced extraction ventilation system. Nearside passenger entry is facilitated by air-operated doors and low step height.   *MAN-VW Truck & Bus*

Rebuilding time. The registration plate to the right is that of YRY 200T, No. 200 in the Leicester City Transport fleet, a Dennis Dominator with East Lancs 76-seat bodywork.   *Colin Peck*

Dead but still useful. A life-expired Bedford OWB with Duple utility bodywork, once DHR 187, after being stripped of all its re-usable components serves well enough as a stores hut.

There was no reason whatsoever why Leyland Motors should not have been proud of their export successes even into the 1980s. This Park Royal bodywork was purpose built for its market, with every window bar one being openable; the ventilators for the driver show the expected conditions although it is surprising (despite the weight penalty) that no air conditioning was included. With 86 seats extra reinforcement of the body was necessary, heavy gauge stress panels being fitted inside both saloons. In all 400 vehicles to the design were supplied and paid for in 1975. *Leyland Truck & Bus*

While crossing Westminster Bridge one lunchtime in 1980 Derek Thomas, the photographer, was surprised to see a bus approaching with Kowloon as its destination. Logically he took some photographs. He was even more surprised when it pulled up, a dragon got out, danced around the machine, climbed back in and the bus moved off. It seems this Volvo Ailsa with Alexander bodywork was the first of a batch and had to be blessed as it crossed water *en route* to the docks. *Derek Thomas*

Clemmed is perhaps the right way to describe both passengers and passers-by, but No. 1470 seen in Preston was an unusual bus insofar as it was used in 1985 for an experiment to replace diesel with Low Pressure Gas. A standard Eastern Coach Works 74-seater body was fitted, but one drawback of the alternative fuel was that heating, always an Achilles' heel of the Atlantean, was conspiciously lacking as evidenced by the upstairs windows. No. 1470 later passed to Cumberland Motor Services (Stagecoach), but with an orthodox Leyland engine.

The ability of bus drivers to continue handling their often clumsy vehicles in the worst of conditions is rarely recorded by the broadcasting media. At a time like this photograph both television and radio will be chattering on about the antics of car drivers seeing a millimetre of snow, not mentioning that the driver of this MCW-bodied Daimler (but Leyland owned by then!) Fleetline had himself to motor in to his garage (Coventry Road, Birmingham) before commencing his driving stint. British Rail staff, when it was British Rail, were obliged to clear platforms of snow before the first train - it is as well that bus companies are under no such obligation as otherwise we know who would have the job ... Incidentally, the advertisement behind the disembarked passenger is 'This little old lady has had arthritis all her life'.

RDA 667R, Midland Red (National Bus Company) fleet No. 667 was a standard 1981 Leyland Leopard PSU3E/4R with Plaxton Supreme Express bodywork and 49 coach (high-backed) seats. She was one of some hundreds of vehicles supplied which met the requirements of the bus grant scheme; this grant (50 per cent of the vehicles' cost) necessitating the use of these vehicles on stage carriage (i.e. bus or express) rather than coach services for the first five years of their lives. These photographs in the Tamworth area, are chosen to show 667 in her proper habitats; in town and country the Leopard was an excellent machine for its period and the Plaxton bodywork, when new, gave reasonable comfort coupled to excellent visibility.

Bus conversions to snack bars are quite commonplace, but what amazes me, as a frequenter of roadside cafes, is just how squalid some of them look. Internally they may be as clean as a new pin, but bearing in mind most of them have to be mobile, if not nomadic, why on earth don't the owners put them through a truck wash from time to time? The Burger Bus, or Eat-in Bus-taurant was found in Blackpool. Hot dogs and burgers were 60p, cheesy double burgers 90p, tea 20p.

The Flying Banana had fallen onto hard times by June 1989. Typical East Lancs bodywork outline on a Leyland chassis but far from 'as delivered'.

Once the pride of Southdown this mobile hospitality bar was laid up in the grounds of a Little Pub Company's premises, the Old Kipper House (now the Red Lion), Feckenham, Worcestershire, in 1993, having last been taxed two years previously.

Bus rallies, gatherings or open days are not an entirely new phenomenon as attendance at the annual Brighton show was almost *de rigeur* for some operators, but gradually changed from being an all-professional exhibition to a chance for 'ordinary' men and women to show off their machines and, equally, for 'ordinary' men and women to come and view them. The locale is often a public park where entrance is free while other rallies incorporate a road run. Some runs will commence in a town and terminate at a museum, while others seek out some local beauty spot or place of interest. Museums sometimes organise these road runs although generally they seem to prefer static exhibitions, while laying on a service of vintage vehicles to the nearest railhead or bus station. These photographs spanning 15 years are merely intended to give the flavour of the days when professional and amateur alike entertain.

PAY·AS YOU ENTER
PLEASE TENDER EXACT FARE

TO OPEN

PHILLIPS COACH CO LTD
SHIPTONTHORPE
EAST YORKSHIRE   UW 6677 K₅₅   TO SEAT 45

PORTREST LTD.
T/A CATTERALLS COACH &
TRAVEL SERVICES
74A COVENTRY ST., SOUTHAM.
LEAMINGTON SPA, WARKS.
Sec. P.R.CATTERALL

J. MORGAN. T/A JOHN'S TRAVEL.
BRYN-OYRE, UPPER COED-CAE,
NANTYGLO, GWENT.

Switch off Heater ondash
When filling fuel tanK

Heater
Fuel   tap off ↘   Fuel tap off ↘

Road Car Services Ltd., The Coachyard, Ashby Rd., Shepshed, Leics
U·W 7874 kgs.   *TO SEAT 51*

CHARNWOOD.COACHES.LTD
THE COACHYARD.ASHBY.RD
SHEPSHED.LEICS

A curious distinction between goods and passenger vehicles can lie in the information displayed. Near our old yard was a tipper operator whose fleet entirely comprised black painted Volvos with no lettering and inevitably obscured number plates, whereas any PSV has to carry the operator's name and registered address 'in clearly legible characters at least 25 mm tall in colours contrasting with their background'. Among other requirements are that all the bodywork and its fittings must be maintained in good serviceable condition and windows must be clean. In London the Metropolitan Police ('Scotland Yard') registration plate was clearly displayed, and always the stop button or petrol cut-off switch must be marked so that they are easily visible seemingly especially for mischevious children's use.

In Vogue - The Mini

Every so often in the history of motor buses someone comes up with another 'Bright Idea'. Usually they are ideas that came before and for a variety of reasons died away. Not entirely surprisingly these ideas are generated for the same reasons as their predecessors and one such was the sudden influx of small, light mini-buses in the 1980s. Like the lightweights of the 1930s they came about as one solution to the joint problems of falling passenger numbers, inability to get round new housing estates due to narrow roads and parked vehicles, the elimination of the necessity to carry a conductor, very low purchase and running costs, and, here today's mini-buses differ from their owner-driver forebears, the training period and expense for new drivers is greatly reduced. Finally, with the Trade Unions weakened by law following their intransigent insistence on the 'right' to strike, wages for mini-bus drivers are often lower than big (or real) bus operators.

The early conversions were based on panel trucks with the shells modified by some of the more respected companies in the PSV body-building industry. Based on mainly Ford Transit, Leyland Sherpa and Mercedes-Benz chassis, by contrast with even Leyland National the earliest batches were pretty dire. While they provided an excellent means of transport for the hitherto house-bound elderly and for housewives on big estates to go shopping in town, they caused problems of their own especially when operating on a five minute or less headway. Within months complaints poured in that they were noisy, smoky, locked up traffic entering and leaving bus stations and that some drivers were none too fussy about driving close to parked cars.

Eventually and realistically none too soon they are being phased out and replaced by the purpose built, comfortable, warm and reliable midi-bus. In many ways the mini has been a victim of its own success as, very often, passenger figures have risen to hitherto unknown heights, but given the short life and high maintenance cost of the mini not every operator has found them a financial success. Often their payload is found to be pathetic, especially on Market day when a relief bus complete with driver and conductor would have to shadow the mini! Now, with small diesels as reliable as full size 'commercial' designs, wage differentials and low prime costs, the minibus heydey seems over as midi-buses enter left . .

Certain types of buses seem to fit into their surroundings like a finger into a well-tailored glove. This is Beaconsfield at a time when retired workmen could sit outside Lloyds Bank without the risk of instant execution by a wayward lorry wheel. The only road sign in the triangle carried the message Slough, and the bus is a Leyland Cub 20-seater with Short Bros of Rochester body, delivered in 1935.

Above: A 1960s Commer/Dodge 2000 with Rootes bodywork being refurbished in 1995 for further work.

Left: In service as a bus to Sherborne and Wincanton in 1995, this 1980 Plaxton Mini-Supreme-bodied Bedford CFL typified the 1960s approach of using parts originally designed for much larger vehicles.

Below: The Cherwell Villager, like a number of its kind relies upon volunteer drivers and quite complex routeing through villages even to remotely pay its way. 'Help the Aged', the Cherwell District Council and the Rural Development Commission were all involved in its operation in 1993.

Above: Midland Red North (one of the constituent parts of the old 'real' Midland Red) operated this Shropshire Bus to Trefonen under the aegis of the Shropshire County Council. The problems for elderly passengers are clear in this view of a No. 303, a 1989 Carlyle-bodied Iveco Daily 49-10S.

Right: A Northern Counties demonstrator on a Renault-Dodge S56 chassis is seen on show in Blackpool, 17th April, 1988.

Below: Chase Bus Services of Chasetown were rightly proud of the coachpainting on their No. 262 E860 WYC; a Dormobile 16-seat Ford Transit VE6 in 1993. The bus was new in 1988.

B55 AOP shown here as West Midlands PTE fleet No. 7055 when new and unlicensed in 1985 was very short-lived being out of the fleet 4 years later. Ford Transits with Carlyle Coachworks 16-seat bodywork, this particular class of minibus proved to be unequal to the demands put on them; apart from being noisy and cramped the lack of ventilation caused the drivers' ears to be severely bent in the summertime! It must be said, however, that elsewhere 'Trannies' generated good passenger traffic, albeit given their short lives not always with as satisfactory a financial return as might be expected.

LKN 585W by contrast utilized the standard Ford Transit body-shell, although in this case it was converted to full PSV specification by the Williams Motor Company of Manchester as a 12-seater (unlike, say, a crewbus which could seat 17 in the same space) but retained the Ford two litre engine.   *Ford Motor Co.*

New Age, New Ways - The 1990s

All these photos were taken between 1993 and 1996 and all show the EEC approved 'Eurobus' sign. The informatio incorporated in them is, however, remarkably varied.

Tywyn

Great Malvern (oddly, Sundays only)

Colwall Green

Taunton

Manchester, Cheetham Hill

Birmingham

Some cities have long since swept away virtually all traces of their history, the few remaining 'old' (i.e. pre-1950) buildings being, as it were, preserved in aspic. Too often though they are crowded out by the brash new concrete glories typical of the post-1960 period. Similarly bus stops and shelters are now often dull, unimaginative, steel and glass advertisement carriers. Here and there are odd survivals, remaining mainly because of inertia and seemingly owned by no-one and thus neglected. Three of these illustrated remained *in situ* 1993, the fourth is all too modern; *above* Great Malvern.

Worcester, still in use during 1996, carrying advertising for a long defunct store. Now refurbished and used as a cycle shed.

Pensive driver watched by two worried Leyland Nationals, Worcester, 1992.

Worcester, detail of redundant shelter.

Coventry, but where does the bus pull up?

Above: One aspect of traffic reduction is the encouragement of road/rail interchange. Unfortunately some of these schemes fell foul of Conservative deregulation, so in Manchester (as just one example) we have buses competing with the very trams which were built to reduce congestion and pollution . . . Madness! In better days, 1990, an OK Travel minibus waits its connection with the Tyne & Wear Metro.

Right: During the extensive replacement works near Birmingham New Street station a 'proper' bus shelter was installed on the forecourt drive. A unique form of road/rail interchange.

Below: Cradley Heath in 1993 and a Midland Red minibus watches the connecting Stourbridge-Birmingham dmu pull away

Above: Buses at bus stops carrying out unusual activities or even 'odd' bus stops are well worthy of inspection. 'Park and Ride' is one of the in phrases; an idea that magically will eliminate congestion in city centres. Given 100 per cent security, warm buses and someone to help load the shopping perhaps this activity might alleviate the problem, but equally should not 'pedestrian precincts' be declared traffic-free instead of, as in most towns, delivery vans and lorries seemingly being allowed to drive through at will? WMPTE effort *c.*1980. The original caption read 'One wonders what would have happened if it had been pouring with rain'.

Colin Peck

Left: Shrewsbury 1995. The bus says it all clearly and whole-heartedly; but the subsidy is heavy.

```
DAYS OF OPERATION: Monday-Friday          START DATE: 30/12/1991

DEPART BROMFORD LANE   DEPOT 0750 AND RUN PRIVATE TO TILE CROSS

    *** The correct blind for Lanchester Way is CHELMSLEY WOOD NORTH ***
```

RTE	TIMING POINT	ARR.	DEP.	RTE	TIMING POINT	ARR.	DEP.
810	TILE CROSS		0805	72E	SOLIHULL STATION		1438
	Marston Green Stn		0808		Sheldon		1452
	The Greenwood		0823		Marston Green Stn		1508
	Chelmsley Wood		0828		CHELMSLEY WOOD	1513	
	Bluebell Drive		0833				
	Coleshill School		0838		Run Private To		
	C.HILL MIDDLE SCH	0843					
				863	C.HILL MIDDLE SCH		1530
	Run Private To				COLESHILL High St	1536	
72	LANCHESTER WAY		0931		Run Private To		
	Kingshurst		0939				
	Chelmsley Wood		0949	810	COLESHILL SCHOOL		1541
	Marston Green Stn		0954		Bluebell Drive		1546
	Sheldon		1010		Chelmsley Wood		1551
72	SOLIHULL STATION	1024	1038		The Greenwood		1556
	Sheldon		1052		Marston Green Stn		1611
	Marston Green Stn		1108		TILE CROSS	1614	
	Chelmsley Wood		1113				
	Kingshurst		1123		Run Private To		
72	LANCHESTER WAY	1130	1131	96	SHIRESTONE ROAD		1708
	Kingshurst		1139		The Mackadown		1711
	Chelmsley Wood		1149		Stechford		1719
	Marston Green Stn		1154		Victoria Street		1728
	Sheldon		1210	96	CARRS LANE	1738	1740
72	SOLIHULL STATION	1224	1238		Victoria Street		1750
	Sheldon		1252		Stechford		1759
	Marston Green Stn		1308		The Mackadown		1807
	Chelmsley Wood		1313		Chelmsley Wood		1816
	Kingshurst		1323	96	BLUEBELL DRIVE	1822	1832
72	LANCHESTER WAY	1330	1331		Chelmsley Wood		1837
	Kingshurst		1339		The Mackadown		1845
	Chelmsley Wood		1349		Stechford		1853
	Marston Green Stn		1354		Victoria Street		1901
	Sheldon		1410		CARRS LANE	1910	
	SOLIHULL STATION	1424					

```
                    - Cont'd -
```

```
Return to depot; Arrive at 1930        Running Board Number:  72-01
```

It is a legal requirement upon operators to publish and 'have readily available' both timetables and fare tables - the latter should be visible inside the saloon although often it is not. A country operator will have a simple timetable with, probably, three daily departures on a route, plus extras on Market Days, alternate Tuesdays or even once a month - this certainly applied to one firm where we ran a service only on the last Sunday in each month. It ran empty. But, apart from these eccentricities the driver will know his route and times by habit, whereas a city man will not as he may work six routes in a week, and be a different time on each. So a 'running board' comes into use. This tells the driver where, what and how the bus is to work. While this particular diagram was officially a two-driver job it was not uncommon for the whole thing to be worked as an overtime incentive. But the lack of meal and 'personal needs' breaks should be noted . . . The relevant fare tables were printed on the reverse as this is an OPO job.

Photographed in 1993 the then Green Bus Service (Warstones Motors) No. 1, WTJ 901L, a Leyland Leopard with rather attractive East Lancs 45-seat bodywork, waits to pull away from Hednesford bus station on the 10.07 service. Once in the fleet of Rossendale the contrast between the almost country run of Route 10 and the hilly work in Lancashire must have seemed unusual even to the bus! Seriously, though, the whole company is run with a mixture of enthusiasm and hard work and the vehicles are usually clean and bright in two-tone green and cream.

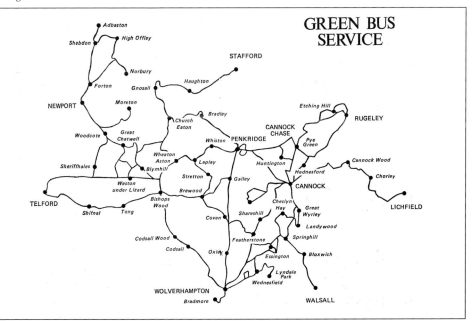

GREEN BUS SERVICE

Two 'Disabled Buses'. The sleek Omni operated from the Royal British Legion, Galanos House, near Long Itchington in 1993. Rather a clever design with a capacity to drop the rear double doors within an inch or two of the ground.

The Mercedes operated by Worcester County Council is more orthodox but has a rear lift and was seen in 1994.

Forlorn on a winter's day in 1994, preserved London Transport Routemaster 1643 and West Midlands Daimler Fleetline 4613 wait side by side for Spring to arrive at Wythall Bus Museum.

Pride of ownership. In 1993 John Godwin purchased XUM 123J from Hillcrest Radio Coaches. A Bedford J2 with modified Plaxton coachwork No. 17 had been laid up for a year or two after some panelling had been replaced prior to re-certification. Unfortunately storage in Surrey proved a problem for John, eventually the vandals smashed most of the glass and XUM finally passed to another owner for conversion to a motor-caravan.

This montage shows 1993 views of what was the old bus and coach station at Euston Road in Morecambe. Once, particularly in summer and specifically during the Wakes Weeks when the whole of the North of England went on holiday, this area was a seething anthill of vehicles, bus crews, harassed Ribble and North Western Road Car inspectors and passengers.

THIS LAND IS THE
PROPERTY OF
RIBBLE MOTOR SERVICES LTD,
AND NO RIGHT OF WAY IS
GRANTED UPON OR OVER
THE SAME.

Passengers coming, going, lost, looking for their children, hungry, irritated and on the way back tearful, quiet or maudlin. The site is now a McCarthy Stone retirement complex. WCK 213Y, then in the fleet of a 'lost' municipal operation, Lancaster City Transport, was a 1982 East Lancs-bodied Leyland Atlantean.

This bus stop opposite the bus station by the Morecambe Bay School remained unchanged in 1997.

Apart from the legal lettering requirements stipulated under various Road Traffic Acts any other paintwork is at the discretion of the operator. Too many vehicles run around with a coat of Dulux white hiding, or trying to hide, previous liveries. As this class of vehicle is too often left unwashed and driven by a fag-end Charlie type of driver such shabbiness does nothing to enhance the industry's image. Conversely as will be apparent in this book, some operators have always shown a delightful awareness of the benefits good paint and clear vinyls can bring; even the much maligned 'Stagecoach stripes' have to be kept clean or they look awful.

Above: The reason for bridge height warnings is evidenced here in 1996 when a PMT (FirstBus) Leyland Olympian became an almost instant open-top bus. The cause of the damage (if not the accident!) is Glebe Street railway bridge at Stoke-on-Trent. *Russell Williams*

Left: In earlier days, January 1984, a fitter was sent up a ladder to check if the clearance was adequate for a Leyland National II. This class of vehicle was subsequently banned from passing under the bridge. *Russell Williams*

A July 1993 photograph that indicates how the whole ethos of transport and travel has changed. The semi-derelict and vandalised station is Scarborough and on the left is a 'Pacer' two-car diesel unit, almost bereft of passengers. The buses are standing on what was once part of an incredibly busy rail-road interchange. Both are empty. The minibus, 'Sorry, not in service', is a 1986 Reeve Burgess-bodied Mercedes Benz of Scarborough & District Motor Service, and the double-decker of Primrose Valley Coaches bound for Reighton Sands is a 1976 MCW-bodied Leyland Fleetline ex-West Midlands PTE.

Right: Kentish Bus & Coach Company's No. 915 was photographed in 1994 acting as a training vehicle. A Bristol LH she was one of five in use including three double-deckers.

John Godwin

Below: Midland Red West Leyland Leopard trainer passes through the wash at Worcester in 1994. The bright yellow colour seems to enhance the lines of the Alexander bodywork.

With a limited number of passenger loading bays available parking facilities are an often overlooked facet of bus station operation. This is Morpeth in 1990 with a mixture of country and town buses waiting their duties. Even here though the Northumbria Motor Services Bristol VRT has 'overflowed'.

Pleased driver - or is that watering can ominous? Near Nuneaton 1992. Bedford CFL with Plaxton Mini-Supreme coach bodywork.

The last photograph in a book can be the hardest to choose, but EUF 204, ex-Brighton Corporation No. 18 seems to typify what can happen to an outworn omnibus. When shiny new in 1938, the chassis came from Leyland classified as type LD5, and was very up to date, this model having only been introduced the previous year. Bodywork was by Park Royal, seating 54 passengers and it says much for the quality of workmanship that the shell still survived in 1990, when found at the West of England Transport Collection, Winkleigh. Park Royal's body factory has long gone, Leyland no longer manufacture buses and the old Brighton Corporation fleet is only a memory.

Acknowledgements

When I was first asked by The Oakwood Press, way back in 1996, to write a companion bus and coach book to my *Glory of Trams* it seemed a simple task, as after all I had been a driver-mechanic and later operator in what were the halcyon days of PSV (or PCV) work. But I rapidly found I had vast holes in my knowledge and it is with great pleasure I acknowledge the help I have received not only from the listed individuals and bodies below but from dozens of other men and women who gave a pointer to the way forward, as well as others who have unconditionally given me permission to use their copyright material. Some, alas, have moved off to Celestial Route No. 1; others I have lost touch with but I thank them all:

J.R. Battersby-Hill; G. Beckett; colleagues at the Birmingham and Midland Museum of Transport, Wythall; Gavin Booth (Glasgow); Gavin Booth, Editor, *Classic Bus*; Roy Brook; Richard Butler; John Carroll of the Crosville Enthusiasts Club; C. Carter; Alan Cross; John E. Dunabin; K.V. Ellis; L.F. Folkard, Hon. Historian, Devon General Society; A.J. Francis; P.R. Gailsbury, Southdown Enthusiasts Club; John Godwin; The Greater Manchester Transport Society (Museum of Transport); G. Harmer; Daniel Hill (Photographer); the late W.J. Haynes; A. Ingram; Malcolm Keeley; R.W. Kidner; Thomas W.W. Knowles, lately MD of Lancaster City Transport; The late Reg Ludgate; The M&D and East Kent Bus Club; J.H. Meredith; Geoff R. Mills; J. Neale; The Omnibus Society, London Historical Research Group; Ken Jubb of the Midlands Branch, Omnibus Society and many other members; Jim Osborne; A.D. Packer; Colin Peck; PSV Circle; G.B. Render; Alan Robinson; C.W. Routh; R.H.G. Simpson; S.W. Stevens-Stratton, Editor, *Vintage Roadscene*; David Stevenson; Chris Taylor; David Taylor; Derek Thomas; Transport Ticket Society; E.V. Trigg; Keith Turns; Russell Williams; Judy-Joan Wright.

Public Libraries, Information Services and Archivists at:

Berwick; Birmingham Local Studies; The Church Army (London); Derby; Holmfirth; Huddersfield; Kingston-upon-Hull; Leeds; Lowestoft; Market Harborough; Stratford-upon-Avon; Warwick; Worcester St Johns Patent Office, Birmingham Public Record Office (London).

I am particularly glad to acknowledge the permission willingly granted to reproduce copyright material held by the following companies:

Evershed & Vignoles; Gabriel & Co.; Gideon Graphics; Ian Allan Publishing Ltd.; Leyland Truck & Bus; Brian Chalke, Lucas Electrical Systems; MAN-VW Truck & Bus; Planet Group plc, Birmingham; J.A. Jones, Stemco Truck Products; Peter Allen of Vintage Racing Cars (AutoVac) Northampton; Voith Engineering Ltd.

Perhaps, unusually, I should add Oakwood Graphics 'layout man' Ian Kennedy, both for surprising me with the news that the book was to proceed and for allowing some author's input into the final choice of illustrations. A rare accolade!

My wife has typed the contents of 29 books so far, contending with changes in machinery from a lovely Hermes manual typewriter to an unloved word processor. As I write all the text, captions, etc., in long-hand she has also had to suffer as my script has deteriorated, busman's knuckles taking its toll. I couldn't do any of it without her.

To write an afterword to a book is always difficult, but my era was typified one glorious summer's day when, as one of them, I took our cricket team to play an invitation match at Scarborough. Ours was a rugged League team, theirs a wandering team of gentlemen, but this was still a time when the England team itself had a marvellous mixture of amateur 'Gentlemen' and professional 'Players'.

Now cricket is a game of pyjamas and 'sledging', and the days of a ride to the coast in a coach all but forgotten. So to paraphrase lines by Francis Thompson (himself writing of a match in his youth) I offer as a requiem:

> Alas, the road is full of cars as I near the shadowy coast,
> And I look through my tears at a petrol-burning host,
> As our ghostly passengers flicker to and fro, to and fro,
> Oh my Leyland and my AEC of long ago, long ago.

Index

Bodybuilders,
  Alexander, 176
  BBW, 81, 107
  Bellhouse, Hartwell, 111
  Birch Bros, 91
  Brush, 59, 63, 84, 86, 87, 106
  Buckingham, 34
  Burlingham, 110, 122
  Carlyle, 186, 187
  Cravens, 56
  Crossley, 86
  DAB, 162
  Dodson, 28
  Dormobile, 186
  Duple, 78, 80, 84, 110, 112,
    113, 119, 124, 126, 143,
    149, 175
  East Lancs, 103, 104, 129,
    147, 156, 158, 175, 179,
    195, 199
  Eastwood & Kenning, 81
  ECW, 105, 136, 146, 147,
    154, 177
  English Electric, 29, 54
  Gabriel & Co., 33
  Garrett, 39
  Goppel, 163
  Great Western Railway, 28
  Gurney Nutting, 87
  Hall Lewis (see also Park
    Royal), 53, 57, 63
  Harrington, 69, 127
  Leyland, 36, 37, 99, 118
  Locomotors, 168
  London Transport (LPTB),
    58 93
  Lydney, 117
  Marshall, 130, 157, 168
  Martin Walter, 144
  Metro-Cammell, inc.
    MCCW/MCW, 62, 80, 85,
    104, 108, 117, 140, 141,
    154, 155, 157, 161, 171,
    173, 177, 201
  Midland Red, 86
  Munnion (Essex), 20
  NCME/Northern Counties,
    41, 140, 156, 167, 186
  North Eastern Railway, 22
  Park Royal, 45, 61, 65, 74,
    75, 81, 85, 90, 111, 121,
    131, 170, 176, 205
  Plaxton, 128, 132, 145, 148,
    178, 185, 197, 204
  Reeve Burgess, 174, 201
  Roe, 84, 95, 101, 118, 125,
    141
  Rootes, 185
  Short Bros, 31, 44, 45, 46, 61,
    184

Bodybuilders (continued),
  Strachans, 48, 116, 119, 123,
    169
  Thomas Tilling 27, 47, 106
  UTA, 102
  Watsons (Lowestoft), 114,
    115
  Weymann, 65, 91, 120, 173
  Williams (Manchester) 187
  Willowbrook, 138, 141, 145,
    149
  Yeates, 87
Locations,
  Alvaston, 14
  Bargoed Hill, 58
  Barnard Castle, 35
  Beaconsfield, 184
  Beamish (Museum), 149
  Birmingham, 86, 148, 171,
    192
  Blackpool, 179, 186
  Boulogne, 30, 31
  Bovey (Devon), 43
  Bradford, 29
  Burnley, 67
  Bury St Edmunds, 42
  Canterbury, 72
  Chagford, 20
  Chasetown, 186
  Coventry, 85 191
  Cradley Heath, 192
  Crawley (Sussex), 145
  Deal, 42
  Douglas (IoM), 69
  Durham, 137
  Eastleigh, 12
  Feckenham (Worcs), 179
  Folkestone, 35
  Frensham Ponds, 119
  Great Malvern, 188, 189
  Hardwick Hall, 149
  Hednesford, 165
  Holmfirth, 40
  Hove, 69
  Huddersfield, 40, 41
  Keighley, 39
  Layer de la Haye, 32
  Leyland, 82
  Liverpool, 15
  London, 14, 15, 17, 24, 25,
    58, 83, 157, 176
  Long Benton, 21
  Lunedale, 145
  Macclesfield, 165
  Maidstone, 43
  Maldon (Essex), 143
  Markfield, 87
  Morecambe, 154, 198, 199
  Morpeth, 203
  Northampton, 84

Locations (continued),
  Nuneaton, 204
  Pillerton Priors, 144
  Prestatyn, 156
  Preston, 177
  Rotherham, 38
  Saltburn by the Sea, 137
  Scarborough, 156, 201
  Sheffield, 166
  Shrewsbury, 193
  Sidmouth, 53
  Solihull, 148
  Southport, 173
  Stafford, 165
  Stoke-on-Trent, 201
  Tamworth, 178
  Tavistock, 67
  Thirsk, 20
  Thornton-le-Dale, 22
  Torquay, 53
  Trefonen, 186
  Wakefield, 49
  Walsall, 85, 140
  West Bromwich, 84
  Winkleigh (Museum), 205
  Wolverhampton, 158
  Worcester, 189, 190, 191, 202
  Worksop, 13
  Wythall (Museum), 166
Chassis manufacturers,
  ADC, 31, 48
  AEC, 27, 28, 50, 58, 61, 62,
    63, 79, 87, 93, 94, 95, 96,
    98, 99, 113, 116, 118, 121,
    126, 127, 130, 131, 141,
    145, 197
  Bedford, 78, 80, 110, 119,
    124, 143, 145, 148, 149,
    157, 168, 169, 175, 185,
    197, 204
  BMC, 144
  Bristol, 65, 81, 105, 107, 136,
    146, 147, 148, 161, 177,
    202, 203
  BUT, 117
  Chevrolet, 66
  Clarkson, 20, 25
  Commer, 31, 90, 185
  Crossley, 86
  Daimler, 34, 54, 55, 56, 78,
    84, 85, 104, 112, 132, 138,
    154, 156, 159, 177, 197
  De Dion Bouton, 21
  Dennis, 175
  Dürkopp, 22
  English Electric, 29
  Ford, 168, 186, 187
  Fordson, 111
  Garrett, 39
  Germain, 23

Chassis manufacturers
   (continued),
Guy, 40, 45, 81, 85, 101, 111,
   121, 123, 125, 140, 158
IVECO, 186
Karrier, 40, 41
Lacoste et Battman, 24
Leyland, 25, 26, 28, 34, 35,
   36, 37, 44, 45, 50, 51, 53,
   58, 65, 67, 74, 75, 76, 77,
   80, 81, 82, 83, 85, 86, 87,
   91, 95, 99, 102, 103, 104,
   106, 108, 110, 117, 118,
   122, 129, 141, 146, 147,
   154, 156, 161, 167, 170,
   172, 173, 176, 179, 180,
   184, 195, 199, 201, 202,
   205
Leyland-DAB, 162
Leyland National (Unitary),
   150, 151, 152, 153, 164, 201
MAN-VW, 163, 175
Maudslay, 59, 60
MCW, 155, 157, 171, 172
Mercedes-Benz, 192, 196,
   201
Mercedes Stoll, 39
Midland Red, 86
Morris-Commercial, 63 69
OMNI, 196
Renault (Dodge), 186
Scott-Stirling, 24
Sentinel, 21
Straker, 38
Thomas Tilling, 27, 79
Thornycroft, 57
Tilling-Stevens, 35, 46, 47,
   106
Operators,
   AA, 101
   Amos, 80
   Batty, 138, 149
   Bedlington & District, 141
   Birmingham, 34, 62, 63, 86,
      99, 112, 158
   Bradford, 29
   Brighton, 205
   Boxall, 66
   Brown's Blues, 78, 87, 94
   Burnley, Colne & Nelson
      (incl. Burnley Corp. and
      Burnley & Pendle), 67, 77,
      103, 104, 129, 146
   Calvary, 149
   Chariot, 50
   Chase Bus Services, 186
   Cherwell DC, 185
   Coventry, 59, 85, 104
   Crosville, 156
   Cumberland MS, 105

Operators (continued),
   Darlington Triumph, 35
   De-luxe, 136
   Devon General, 52
   Doncaster, 95
   East Kent, 35, 43, 47, 69, 72,
      74, 75, 76, 81, 106, 111, 121
   East Midland, 118
   Express (Partridge), 25, 51
   Frakes 66
   Great Western Railway, 12,
      28, 43
   Green Bus Service, 195
   Highland Transport, 123
   Hillcrest, 197, 204
   Huddersfield, 40, 41
   Keighley, 39
   Kentish Bus, 202
   Kingston-upon-Hull, 140
   Inner London EA, 168
   Isle of Man RS, 69
   Jenkins (Newport), 110
   Johnston, Thomas, 100
   Lancaster City, 154, 199
   Ledgard, 95
   Leicester, 175
   Leigh, 117
   Lewisham BC, 169
   LGOC, 14, 17, 27
   London and South Western
      Railway, 20
   London General, 172
   London Power Omnibus, 24
   London Road Car, 25
   London Transport (LPTB),
      58, 73, 92, 93, 94, 96, 97,
      98, 99, 141, 155, 157, 184
   Maidstone & District, 46
   Manchester, 155
   Mexborough & Swinton, 39
   Midland Red (BMMO), 77,
      86, 103, 178
   Midland Red (North), 163,
      186, 192
   Midland Red (West), 202
   Moffit (Hexham), 105
   Morecambe & Heysham, 61
   Newcastle-upon-Tyne, 21,
      117
   Newport, 173
   Northampton, 84, 159
   North Eastern Railway, 20,
      22
   Northumbria, 203
   North Western Road Car,
      106, 141
   Nottingham, 161, 167
   OK Travel, 192
   Osborne's (Tollesbury), 142,
      143

Operators (continued),
   PMT, 129, 173, 201
   Pontypridd UDC, 81
   Primrose Valley, 201
   Red & White, 108
   Renown, 51
   Ribble MS, 122, 177
   Rotherham, 38
   Royal British Legion, 196
   St Helens, 118
   Saltburn MS, 137
   Scarborough & District, 201
   Scarlet Band, 137
   Seagull, 110
   Sheffield, 133
   Shropshire Playbus
      Association, 170
   SMT, 80
   Southampton, 147
   Southdown, 86, 179
   Southend-on-Sea, 112
   South Wales, 130, 131, 147
   South Yorkshire PTE, 154,
      162, 163
   Stanhope MS, 101
   Stockton, 56, 120
   Summerskill, 50
   Thomas Tilling, 16
   Trent, 134, 135
   Trimdon MS, 149
   United Counties, 28 156
   UTA, 102
   Venture Transport
      (Newcastle), 138, 139
   Wallasey, 54, 108, 173
   Walsall, 85
   Waltham Forest BC, 168
   West Bromwich, 84
   Western National, 67
   West Hartlepool, 73
   West Midlands PTE, 171,
      172, 177, 187, 193
   West Mon OB, 58
   West Riding, 49, 125
   Windsorian, 78
   Wolverhampton, 140, 158
   Worksop & Retford
      Brewery, 13
Patents, 18, 19
Tickets, 19, 31, 53, 70, 71, 88, 89
Timetables, 52, 100, 134, 135,
   142, 194